A book loan to help you with the loss of your loved one from:

VISTACARE
FOUNDATION

The VistaCare Foundation is a non-profit organization working to enhance the quality of life for those with life-limiting illnesses and their loved ones. We do this through memorial gifts and bequests from people who share our mission and compassion.

Our mission is accomplished by bestowing grants in three areas of need:

Providing essentials or "last wishes" to needy hospice patients so they may live their last days in peace and comfort, surrounded by the love of family and friends.

Educating healthcare professionals about the wonderful benefits of hospice care that are available for their patients.

Funding research to expand the availability and improve the services of hospice and end-of-life care.

For information on how you can help, please contact the VistaCare Foundation toll-free at 1-877-478-4782. You can also visit your local VistaCare office.

REVISED EDITION

The Grief Recovery *Handbook*

THE ACTION PROGRAM FOR MOVING BEYOND DEATH, DIVORCE, AND OTHER LOSSES

JOHN W. JAMES

AND RUSSELL FRIEDMAN

HarperPerennial

A Division of HarperCollinsPublishers

HarperCollins books may be purchased for educational, business, or sales promotional use. For information please write: Special Markets Department, HarperCollins Publishers, Inc., 10 East 53rd Street, New York, NY 10022.

FIRST EDITION

Designed by Elina D. Nudelman

Library of Congress Cataloging-in-Publication Data

James, John W.
     The grief recovery handbook : the action program for moving beyond death, divorce, and other losses / John W. James and Russell Friedman.—Rev. ed.
     p. cm.
     ISBN 0–06–095273–3 (paperback)
     ISBN 0–06–019279–8 (hardcover)
     1. Grief. 2. Loss (Psychology) I. Friedman, Russell.
II. Title.
BF575.G7J36   1998
152.8—dc21   98-16555

98 99 00 01 02 ❖/RRD 10 9 8 7 6 5 4 3 2 1

For the son I never knew.—J.W.J.

For my mom—you were my champion!—R.F.

And to all of you who are moving beyond loss.

Contents

Introduction

It is unlikely that a person would wake up one morning and say, "Grief, what a concept, I think I'll make it my life's work." That is not how it happened for either of us. We are John W. James and Russell Friedman, and together we represent the Grief Recovery Institute.

Here is a little outline of our lives, the institute, and the evolution of *The Grief Recovery Handbook*.

John was thrust painfully into this arena by the death of a child in 1977. After discovering a successful process for completing his grief, he continued his career in the solar energy design business. Acquaintances who had heard of his loss and recovery experience brought their friends who were dealing with loss. Soon John was spending as much time with grievers as with contractors, and finding his work with the former more rewarding. After a while, he realized that grief recovery was what he was meant to do. As a direct result of John's awareness, the Grief Recovery Institute was established.

Russell's introduction to grief recovery came not as the

result of a death but in response to a second divorce coupled with a bankruptcy. He never would have equated his circumstances with the word *grief* had he not been dragged to a lecture on grief recovery presented by John. At that lecture Russell realized that there might be a solution for his overwhelmingly painful feelings. The following day, he showed up at the Grief Recovery Institute as a volunteer. Ten years later, he is still there.

The Grief Recovery Institute has been guided by a primary principle, *to deliver grief recovery assistance to the largest number of people in the shortest period of time*. To meet this goal, the institute established Outreach Programs throughout the United States and Canada. Feedback from those fledgling support groups indicated a clear need for additional support. The first version of *The Grief Recovery Handbook* was written and self-published to meet that demand. The success of the book made it clear that a mainstream publisher might be able to extend our reach and help even more grievers.

In 1988 HarperCollins (then Harper & Row) agreed to publish an updated edition, ensuring that many more grievers would have access to effective help in overcoming loss. This has been a very successful collaboration. The nationwide wing span of HarperCollins has helped *The Grief Recovery Handbook* become available in every community, large and small. With availability has come recovery.

There is no accurate way to determine how many people have been helped by the two previous editions of *The Grief Recovery Handbook*. Conservative estimates would indicate that the number is more than half a million people. While we are excited and pleased to have the chance to update the handbook, we must begin by acknowledging and thanking all of you who were responsible for the success of the earlier ones.

We want to give special recognition to the thousands of grieving people who have shared their lives through their calls and
letters. It is your feedback and input that have encouraged us
to make the changes that in turn will help many more hurting
people. We also want to acknowledge the thousands of professionals who have embraced our work. Your suggestions
and encouragement have been invaluable.

And now, *The Grief Recovery Handbook, Revised Edition.*

In the ten years following the 1988 edition, we have made
tremendous strides in helping grieving people. This revised
edition allows us to pass along to the reader all of the
improved actions that lead to recovery. The new material in
this edition is added to support the original idea that, "*with
correct information and correct choices, a person can recover from
any significant emotional loss.*"

We have lectured and consulted for every imaginable type of
organization—universities, medical schools, hospitals, alcohol
and drug rehabilitation programs, funeral homes and ceme-
teries, public and private schools, as well as social, religious,
and philosophical groups—throughout the world. While this
list may be academically impressive, we would like you to dis-
regard it. *Although the list is intellectually accurate, it is emotionally irrelevant.*

As our personal stories illustrate, we did not come to our
careers in grief recovery by way of intellectual pursuit. We
were jolted into this work by our broken hearts. Every one of
you arrives at this book because your heart has been broken
too. While you already know your heart is broken, your question might be, "What do I do about it?" This book has the
answer. The concepts of grief recovery presented here represent a breakthrough in helping grieving people deal success-
fully with loss.

Most professionals have addressed grief from a conceptual, intellectual perspective. *This has often left grievers with much understanding—but very little recovery.* This book is focused totally on recovery from the emotional pain caused by death, divorce, and other losses.

For all of you struggling with unresolved grief issues, we know that the actions outlined in this book will lead you to completion of the pain caused by loss. We also know that recovery is not an easy journey. We know that your losses may have closed your heart down. If we could, we would be with you as you take the actions that will lead your heart to open again. You may be afraid to start, or you may get scared along the way. Please remember that hundreds of thousands of people have used these same actions. We know that they join us in encouraging you to move through your apprehension and begin the process of recovery.

We wish you good luck on your journey, and remain,
Of service,

John & Russell

The Grief Recovery Handbook

PART ONE

Seeing the Problem

If you are reading this book, there is a high probability that your heart is broken.

It may have been caused by a death, either recent or long ago.

It may have been caused by a divorce or the breakup of a romantic relationship.

It may have been caused by any of the more than forty other losses that a person can encounter during a lifetime.

It could be caused by an awareness that your life is not as happy or fulfilling as you want it to be.

Regardless of the cause of your broken heart, you know how you feel, and it probably isn't good.

We are not going to tell you how you feel. You already know. And we will not tell you, "We know how you feel," because we don't. *Neither does anyone else.* At best, we remember how we felt when our losses occurred.

Even though you've endured painful changes in the circumstances of your life, we are going to tell you what actions you need to take to regain a sense of well-being.

HOW TO USE *THE GRIEF RECOVERY HANDBOOK*

Don't jump ahead in your reading of this handbook. There is a difference between those who resolve their pain and those who don't. The ones who recover follow a well-defined plan. We want you to follow such a plan so that you can be successful.

This handbook is designed to give you the information necessary to recover from loss. It has much to offer anyone who truly wants to feel better. It will allow you to choose *completion* and *recovery* rather than *isolation* and *avoidance*. If you use it, one word at a time, it will accelerate your recovery tenfold.

Throughout the text are suggestions, notes, and guidelines. Please don't take any shortcuts. They can lead you unwittingly right back to old ideas that still won't work. Stay on track with this program and with your recovery.

WARNING

This book is not intended as a teaching manual, so we alert you to avoid the temptation of thinking that reading this book or taking the actions in it prepares you to help others. We offer very specific Grief❣Recovery® Certification Programs for that purpose. At the back of the book are addresses and phone numbers to use in contacting us for more information about all of our programs.

1

Grief: A Neglected and Misunderstood Process

Grief is the normal and natural reaction to loss of any kind. Therefore, the feelings you are having are also normal and natural for you. The problem is that we have all been socialized to believe that these feelings are abnormal and unnatural.

While grief is normal and natural, and clearly the most powerful of all emotions, it is also *the most neglected and misunderstood experience, often by both the grievers and those around them.*

Grief is the conflicting feelings caused by the end of or change in a familiar pattern of behavior. What do we mean by *conflicting feelings?* Let us explain by example. When someone you love dies after suffering a long illness, you may feel a sense of relief that your loved one's suffering is over. That is a positive feeling, even though it is associated with a death. At the same time, you may realize that you can no longer see or touch that person. This may be very painful for you. These conflicting feelings, relief and pain, are totally normal in response to death.

What about divorce? Are there conflicting feelings too? Yes. You may feel a genuine sense of freedom now that the battles are over. That is a positive feeling. At the same time, you may be afraid that you will never "find someone as beautiful/as good a provider." These conflicting feelings, freedom and fear, are also natural responses to loss.

All relationships have aspects of familiarity whether they are romantic, social, familial, or business. What other losses cause similar conflicting feelings? While death and divorce are obvious, many other loss experiences have been identified that can produce grief. Among them are:

> Death of a pet
> Moving
> Starting school
> Death of a former spouse
> Marriage
> Graduation
> End of addictions
> Major health changes
> Retirement
> Financial changes—positive or negative
> Holidays
> Legal problems
> Empty nest

Often these common life experiences are not seen as grieving events. We grieve for the loss of all relationships we deem significant—which are thus also emotional.

If the major loss events in your life have not been associated with death, do not put this book down.

After twenty years of working with grievers, we have identified several other losses, including loss of trust, loss of safety, and loss of control of one's body (physical or sexual abuse). Society still does not recognize these losses as grief issues.

Loss-of-trust events are experienced by almost everyone and can have a major, lifelong negative impact. You may have experienced a loss of trust in a parent, a loss of trust in God, or a loss of trust in any other relationship. Is loss of trust a grief issue? The answer is *yes*. And the problem of dealing with the grief it causes remains the same. Grief is normal and natural, but we have been ill prepared to deal with it. *Grief is about a broken heart, not a broken brain.* All efforts to heal the heart with the head fail because the head is the wrong tool for the job. It's like trying to paint with a hammer—it only makes a mess.

Almost all intellectual comments are preceded by the phrase, "Don't feel bad." In 1977, when John's infant son died, a well-meaning friend said, "Don't feel bad—you can have other children." The intellectually accurate statement that John had the physical capability to have other children was not only irrelevant, it was unintentionally abusive, because it belittled his natural and normal emotions. John felt bad, his heart was broken.

When Russell and his first wife divorced, he was devastated. A friend said, "Don't feel bad—you'll do better next time." Most of the comments that grievers hear following a loss, while intellectually accurate, are emotionally barren. As a direct result of these conflicting ideas, a griever often feels confused and frustrated, feelings that lead to emotional isolation.

Since most of us have been socialized to attempt to resolve all issues with our intellect, grief remains a huge problem.

This intellectual focus has even led to academic articles that suggest gender is an issue in grief. We recognize that males and females are socialized differently, but our experience indicates that males and females are similarly limited when it comes to dealing with sad, painful, and negative feelings. Feelings themselves are without gender. There is no such thing as girl sad or boy sad, girl happy or boy happy.

We are not saying that intellect is totally useless in regard to grief. In fairness, you are reading a book, which is an intellectual activity. The book will ask you to understand concepts and to take actions, so clearly there is a degree of intellect involved.

GRIEF AND RECOVERY

For many, seeing this book's title is the first time they have ever seen the terms "grief" and "recovery" used together. Religious and spiritual leaders have pointed out for centuries that we should look at loss as an opportunity for personal spiritual development. Yet in modern life, moving through intense emotional pain has become such a misunderstood process that most of us have very little idea of how to respond to loss.

What do we mean by recovery? Recovery means feeling better. Recovery means claiming your circumstances instead of your circumstances claiming you and your happiness. Recovery is finding new meaning for living, without the fear of being hurt again. Recovery is being able to enjoy fond memories without having them precipitate painful feelings of regret or remorse. Recovery is acknowledging that it is perfectly all right to feel sad from time to time and to talk about those feelings no matter how those around you react. Recovery is being able to forgive others when they say or do things that you know are based on their lack of knowledge about grief. Recovery is one day realizing that your ability to talk about the loss you've experienced is indeed normal and healthy.

Most important, recovery means acquiring the skills that we should have been taught in childhood. These skills allow us to deal with loss directly. Most of us are aware that there is no guarantee that our loved ones will be alive when we get home. Those who have experienced divorce also realize there is no guarantee that our spouse will love us when we get home. The skills of grief recovery will heal your heart if it gets broken and in turn allow you to participate 100 percent in all of your relationships. With the knowledge and freedom brought about by completing losses comes the additional benefit of allowing ourselves to love as totally as possible.

Obviously, recovering from a significant emotional loss is not an easy task. Taking the actions that lead to recovery will require your attention, open-mindedness, willingness, and courage.

STAYING OPEN TO GRIEF

We've all heard the statement, "The only things certain in life are death and taxes." Those of you who are reading this book know that one more item must be added to these certainties: loss. We all experience loss many times in our lives. Despite the universality of the experience of loss, people know very little about recovery from it.

What we do know about grievers is that they've always

wanted to recover. They seek help from all available sources. Grievers attend support groups, read pamphlets, buy books. After having done all these things, they're still confronted with the fact that our entire society is ill equipped to help them bring the grieving experience to a successful conclusion. Over time the pain of unresolved grief is cumulative. Whether caused by a death, divorce, or other type of loss, incomplete recovery can have a lifelong negative impact on a person's capacity for happiness.

GRIEF RECOVERY: HOW DOES IT WORK?

Recovery from loss is achieved by a series of small and correct choices made by the griever.

Sadly, most of us have not been given the necessary information with which to make correct choices. This book takes on the specific challenge of reeducating anyone who has a genuine desire to discover and complete the emotional pain caused by loss. We know that the principles discussed here work. They work for those who have experienced the death of a loved one, a divorce, or any other loss.

The death of a loved one produces emotions that can be described as *the feeling of reaching out for someone who has always been there, only to find that when we need them one more time, they are no longer there.*

Some of you will be reading this book for help in dealing

with a problematic relationship with someone who has died. We might call this a relationship with a "less than loved one." For you, the feeling is one of *reaching out for someone who has never been there for you, and still isn't.* This is also true for those of you who need to discover and complete the unfinished emotions attached to a living person with whom you have a less than fulfilling relationship.

It is almost always true that loss as a result of divorce falls into the "less than loved one" category. Although divorce severs the marital, sexual, and social ties, *divorce does not complete emotional ties.* Without successful recovery, it is common for divorcés—male and female—to repeat their mistakes in ensuing relationships.

AN INCOMPLETE PAST MAY DOOM THE FUTURE

We have no moral, legal, religious, or social position about divorce. We have a very simple belief that everyone involved in a divorce is a griever. That includes children, parents, siblings, and friends of the couple. This attitude makes it easy for us. We always know that the primary issue is unresolved grief.

Divorce (or a broken romantic relationship) produces grief. This can become a life-limiting reality that negatively affects future relationships. Incomplete grief over a former spouse will dictate fearful choices. Incomplete grief will create hypervigilant self-protection from further emotional pain. Sadly, this excess of caution limits the ability to be open, trusting, and loving, dooming the next relationship to failure.

We hope you will recognize the need to go back and complete prior relationships in order to enhance the possibility of success in your current one. For those of you still feeling isolated and alone, we hope this book gives you the courage to complete prior relationships so you can venture forth into the world and seek a new, healthy romantic relationship.

2

Compounding the Problem

Grief is difficult enough without added complications. Unfortunately, many factors can compound our reactions to loss and limit our recovery. This chapter will alert you to some of the pitfalls that can stall or short-circuit your recovery.

CONFUSION ABOUT STAGES

Many people are familiar with the pioneering work of Dr. Elisabeth Kubler-Ross, who identified five emotional stages that a dying person may go through after being diagnosed with a terminal illness. She identified those stages as denial, anger, bargaining, depression, and acceptance.

One result of Dr. Kubler-Ross's work is that many people now tend to apply the concept of stages to other aspects of human emotion. Grief, which follows death, divorce, and other losses, should not, however, be regarded in terms of stages. The nature and intensity of feelings caused by a loss relate to the individuality and uniqueness of the relationship.

While Dr. Kubler-Ross's contributions brought heightened awareness about the process of *dying,* her work has been accompanied by some unfortunate collateral damage. Many people, professionals and the general public alike, have attempted to apply her stages to the emotions that arise after a loss. She identified denial as the first stage that follows notification of a terminal illness. Absent other helpful information, her work has often been misinterpreted to imply that denial is also a stage that a person experiences following a death or divorce.

In all our years working with grievers, we have yet to be approached by someone who is in "denial" that a loss had occurred. The very first thing they say to us is, "My mother died," or, "My dog died," or, "My wife divorced me." These statements reflect absolutely no denial that a loss has occurred. If you are reading this book, *you are not in denial* that you have experienced a loss.

WHAT ABOUT ANGER?

Much of the literature about grief contends that anger is always a factor in loss. Respectfully, we disagree. Anger is sometimes associated with the circumstances of a loss. It is often a factor in our difficult relationships with less than loved ones. Yet the presumption of anger is both incorrect and dangerous. A death often involves no anger at all. One brief account illustrates the point.

"My ninety-two-year-old grandmother, with whom I had a wonderful relationship, became ill and died. Blessedly, it happened quickly, so she did not suffer very much. I am pleased about that. I had just spent time with her and told her how much I cared about her. I am very happy about that. There was a funeral ceremony that accurately portrayed her. Many people came and talked about her. I loved that. At the funeral, a helpful friend reminded me to say good-bye. I did and am glad. I am not angry."

This is a true story. If the story had been different, it would have created different feelings. If the grandson had not been able to talk to his grandmother before she died, he might have been angry at the circumstances that prevented him from doing so. If she had been a less than loved one, he might have been angry that she died before he had a chance to repair the relationship.

Please do not believe that anger is an automatic part of unresolved grief. Some grievers will be angry, and others won't. But if anger is there, we will find it and complete it.

COMMON RESPONSES

While there are no stages of grief, many grievers do experience some very common responses.

Reduced concentration. A griever is in the bedroom. He has an idea about getting something from the kitchen. Upon arrival in the kitchen, he has no earthly idea why he is there or what he went there to get. A preoccupation with the emotions of loss and an inability to concentrate seem to be universal responses to grief.

A sense of numbness. Grievers typically report to us that the first reaction they experience after notification of a loss is a sense of numbness. This numbness can be physical, emotional, or both. The numbness lasts a different length of time for each person. Rarely have we seen this sense of numbness last more than several hours. This reaction is often mislabeled as denial.

Disrupted sleep patterns. Grievers report either not being able to sleep or sleeping too much—or both, alternately.

Changed eating habits. Grievers tell us that they have no appetite or that they eat nonstop—or both, alternately.

Roller coaster of emotional energy. Grievers talk about going up and down and in and out of feelings. As a direct result of these emotional highs and lows, grievers often feel emotionally and physically drained. This reaction will be discussed in depth later in the book.

These are all normal and natural responses to loss. Their duration is unique to every individual. We will not predict for you how long they should last. They do not always occur. They are not stages.

There are no stages of grief. But people will always try to fit themselves into a defined category if one is offered to them. Sadly, this is particularly true if the offer comes from a powerful authority such as a therapist, clergyperson, or doctor.

Do not allow anyone to create any time frames or stages for you.

There are no absolutes in grief. There are no reactions so universal that all, or even most, people will experience

**them. There is only one unalterable truth: All relationships
are unique.**

GETTING OVER OR GETTING COMPLETE

One of the most damaging pieces of misinformation is the
idea that you can "never get over" the death of a child. This
absolutely incorrect claim is made to parents whose child has
died, but it is also made in connection with other losses.
Grieving parents and others then seek out information and
emotions to match the untruth.

It is more accurate to ask, "Is it possible to forget your child
or, for that matter, your spouse or parent?" Clearly the answer
is no! "Not forgetting" becomes incorrectly entangled with
the idea of "not getting over." This crippling idea keeps the
griever's heart eternally broken, does not allow for recovery of
any kind, and, more often than not, severely limits any fond
memories associated with the relationship.

Last January we were talking with a woman whose daughter had committed suicide in the month of February several
years earlier. As we talked, she told us that as February
approached, she thought about her daughter more and more.
Many of her thoughts and feelings were painful. We
acknowledged the truth of her feelings and the logic of the
renewed intensity as the painful anniversary date neared. Her
eyes welled up with tears as she talked about her relationship
with her daughter. She said, "My heart is permanently broken."

Most people would accept her comment and move on. But

we didn't. Instead, we asked her whether she often had fond memories of her daughter. She said yes. We asked how she felt when those fond and pleasant memories came to mind. She said they felt good. So we asked, "When you are having pleasant memories, does your heart feel broken?" "No," she said, "it doesn't."

We then suggested that she not use the phrase "permanently broken heart" to describe herself. We recommended that she say instead, "Sometimes when I am reminded of her struggles and her death, my heart feels broken. Other times, remembering her wonderful qualities, I feel happy and pleased to share my memories about her."

There is a common and false picture created by grievers, by professionals, and by the literature: "Because I haven't forgotten her and still sometimes have feelings about her, I am not over the pain of the loss." This tragic setup is guaranteed to restrict and deflate the life of the griever.

WHEN IS IT TIME TO BEGIN TO RECOVER?

Earlier we mentioned that a sense of numbness and a reduced ability to concentrate are typical for grievers. In spite of those responses, grievers are willing to *talk about the circumstances of the loss* and to *review the relationship they had.* (This review occurs with all losses.) Consequently, effective grief recovery can begin almost immediately. It is very easy to tap into that review and discover a multitude of undelivered emotional communications. Even the most loving and complete of relationships will end with some incompleteness.

The accuracy of our memories is heightened by the loss itself. This can be an ideal opportunity to harvest an incredible collection of memories. Grievers need and want to talk about their losses. It is typical for a family to talk immediately afterwards about the family member who died. It is equally common following a divorce, retirement, pet loss, job loss, or physical change to talk about the good and bad experiences within those relationships or events.

Talking about loss and about relationships is wonderful and good, but it is generally not enough to allow us to feel complete. We need to take additional actions to help complete the pain we discover as we talk about our relationships.

One of our saddest experiences involves people who have signed up to participate in a Grief Recovery Seminar or a Grief Recovery Outreach Program but don't appear at the session. Occasionally, they call to cancel saying, "My therapist said I'm not ready to do my grief work yet."

Here is a little two-part quiz that graphically answers the question, "When do I begin to recover?"

1. If you fell down and gashed your leg and blood was pouring out, would you immediately seek medical attention? The obvious answer is yes.
2. If circumstances and events conspired to break your heart, would you seek attention immediately, or would you allow yourself to bleed to death emotionally? Pick one!

Is it ever too soon to begin to recover? *No.* The first ten years of our grief recovery careers were devoted to helping funeral directors, cemeterians, and clergy better assist grieving people. Clearly, those professionals are helping grievers in the hours and days immediately following a death. *It is never too soon to address your grief.*

SUICIDE, MURDER, AIDS, AND OTHER
TRAGIC CIRCUMSTANCES

Emotional isolation is a major problem for grievers. Focusing on the cause of a loss, such as suicide, murder, AIDS, or another tragic circumstance, tends to increase this isolation.

Grief is by definition emotional. That is not to say that the cause of death does not generate emotion. Clearly, if someone we love dies in tragic circumstances, we will have volumes of feeling about the unfairness of it all. After acknowledging that we have been affected by the circumstances of a death, we must move immediately toward two larger truths.

The first is a painful question. Would you miss your loved one any less if he or she had died some other way? The answer is always *no*.

And second, what is left emotionally unfinished for you as the result of this death?

Earlier we talked about *anger* and *denial* not being helpful words for grievers. Closure is another unhelpful and inaccurate word. Following jury verdicts, the media rush in, thrusting cameras and microphones in grievers' faces. They ask whether the decision has brought "closure." The answer is always *no*.

Lawsuits may or may not serve justice. When the suit is over, however, you are still left with what is emotionally unfinished between yourself and your loved one who has died. At best, the lawsuit completes the crime or the infraction. A lawsuit cannot help you become *emotionally complete*.

We have seen people make a life cause out of the circumstances that took their loved one. We find nothing wrong with that. All of us in society benefit from heightened awareness and increased oversight regarding the law, medicine, and other issues. Our lives are enhanced by the tireless efforts of these reformers. Sadly, though, most of them remain incomplete with their loved one who died. Their tremendous expenditure of energy keeps them constantly distracted from the primary issue, their own unresolved grief.

Some of you will have cause to pursue lawsuits, either civil or criminal, relating to the death or mistreatment of a loved one. We encourage you to do the actions of grief recovery first. Completion will make you a better advocate. You will have more energy. Most important, you will not operate under the illusion that a lawsuit or judgment will heal your broken heart.

THE "G" WORD

An often misused word applied to grief is *guilt*. At the Grief Recovery Institute, we call it the "G" word. We almost never introduce that word to grievers, because it is rarely the right word.

A standard painful interaction at the Grief Recovery Institute sounds like this:

GRIEVER: My son committed suicide. I feel so guilty.
INSTITUTE: Did you ever do anything with intent to harm your son?
GRIEVER: No. (*This is an almost universal response.*)
INSTITUTE: The dictionary definition of guilt implies intent to harm. Since you had no intent to harm, can you put the "G" word back in the dictionary? You are probably devastated enough by the death of your son, you don't need

to add to it by hurting yourself with an incorrect word that distorts your feelings.

GRIEVER: Really? I never thought of it that way.

INSTITUTE: Are there some things that you wish had ended *different, better, or more*?

GRIEVER: Oh, yes.

And then the floodgates open.

In rare instances, people have done things with intent to harm. When that is true, an apology helps to remove any obstacles to completion.

SURVIVOR: ANOTHER INACCURATE WORD

You may have noticed that throughout this book, you have not seen the word *survivor*. This is intentional. *Survivor* is intellectually accurate. It implies that the griever has outlived someone else. But we have discovered that the word *survivor* tends to act as both a definition and a diagnosis and often keeps people stuck in a dangerous and painful rut. For example, you don't survive someone else's suicide. You may survive if someone tries to murder you, but not when they attempt or commit suicide.

More important, the word *survivor* defines the griever and causes him or her to constantly revisit the circumstances about the loss. Being a survivor often becomes an identity. The strong, habituated identification with pain can become who the griever is. It is not uncommon for grievers to get more caught up in defining themselves and their pain than in completing the unfinished emotional aspects of the relationship. All the while, they are liable to remain incomplete with the person who died.

We know there are groups organized around and limited to those who have experienced specific losses, such as suicide, murder, AIDS, death of a child, and even divorce. Since we believe that grievers are already isolated in our society, we also believe that segregating grievers by *type of loss* adds to that isolation. However, we recognize that meeting together with others who have had a similar experience is not without its comforts.

Our beliefs, confirmed by twenty years of hands-on experience, are that:

> All relationships are unique; therefore all recovery is individual.
> Focusing on the shared intellectual truth (type of loss) does nothing to promote the process of recovery.
> Isolation by type of loss may have short-term value but does not encourage long-term solutions.

THERE IS NOTHING WRONG WITH YOU

Major losses resulting from death, divorce, and other causes are usually not common occurrences. Therefore, we are generally not familiar with the thoughts and feelings we experience following losses. It is inevitable that we fall back on whatever information we have learned in the past to try to deal with our responses to the conflicting feelings caused by a loss event. Throughout this book, we refer to the fact that most of us were socialized incorrectly on the topic of grief. However, nothing we say here is intended in any way to condemn society, anyone's parents, or any institutions. We do not believe that one generation intentionally hands down misinformation to the next. We believe that people teach what they know, which is most likely what they were taught.

If you have found that the available information and support have not been adequate in helping you recover from loss, it is not because of what's wrong with you—it's because there is a lack of correct information. If you're reading this book, it means you're open to your grief. It means you're open to beginning a process of recovery that will enhance your life rather than limit it. If you're reading this book, it's because of what's right with you, not what's wrong.

3

We Are Ill Prepared to Deal with Loss

Shortly after the loss you experienced, you probably became acutely aware of how ill prepared you were to deal with the conflicting mass of emotions we call grief. The same is true for almost everyone in our society. We are far better prepared to deal with minor accidents than we are to deal with grief. We receive more education about simple first aid than we do about death, divorce, and other emotional losses.

Stop and consider your own experience. In grade school, you took a class on first aid; in high school, you took a class on health and safety. The local Red Cross offers classes on first aid in the community. Nationwide we have a convenient 911 number to call in case of emergency. At some level, we're all prepared to take action if an accident occurs in our presence. How many classes have you taken on how to deal with the grief caused by significant emotional loss?

We think it's strange that we all know what to do if someone breaks an arm, but very few people are prepared to assist grievers. Eight million people become new grievers each year owing to death alone. In addition, the divorce rate exceeds 45 percent. This statistic does not include relationships that were never formalized by marriage. Many millions of relationships end annually, affecting not only the couple but children, parents, other relatives, and friends. It is estimated that more than fourteen million pets die per year in the United States alone. When you add the many millions of loss experiences related to retirement, job loss or change, medical problems, and major financial changes, the numbers are staggering.

WE'RE TAUGHT HOW TO ACQUIRE THINGS, NOT WHAT TO DO WHEN WE LOSE THEM

In our formative years, an overwhelming emphasis is placed on learning how to acquire things in order to make life successful and happy.

In early childhood, we try to acquire our parents' praise. Later we try to acquire toys at Christmas or Hanukkah by being good. We try to earn high grades in school in order to gain approval. We try to look attractive to our peers so we'll be accepted. This process of learning how to acquire objects and attention continues into our adult lives. Certainly the advertising industry understands this phenomenon: marketing campaigns focus on finding happiness and contentment through the acquisition of things.

While we have learned much about acquiring things, we have precious little accurate information on what to do when we lose them.

Loss is inevitable. Sometimes loss is even predictable. In spite of these truths, we receive no formal training in how to respond to events that are guaranteed to happen and sure to cause pain and disruption. We are even advised not to learn about dealing with loss—or at the very least, not to talk about it. "What's done is done." "You have to move on." "Don't burden others with your feelings." The list goes on and on.

We are all liable to face several major losses in our lives. We must acknowledge that much of what we've learned about processing the feelings caused by loss is incorrect. In fact, if we had no knowledge about dealing with grief, we would be better off than we are operating with what we currently know. Most of us rely on old ideas to deal with whatever crisis confronts us. Even though we could show you that most of the ideas you learned about dealing with grief are not helpful, you may fall back on them when faced with the painful thoughts and feelings caused by loss. We typically do the same actions the same way, over and over. All actions, physical and emotional, become habitual. This is actually good news, being able to develop and maintain habits. The crucial step is to develop some helpful habits for dealing with grief.

First, in order to develop a new habit, you must become aware of the need to have a new habit. If you are reading this book, you are probably already aware that you need more effective information and habits for dealing with grief. Second, you must learn the component parts or skills necessary to build the habit. In the case of grief, this means identifying the ideas that do not work and replacing them with ideas that do. Third, you must practice the new ideas so that you can turn them into habits.

As you work your way through this book, you will be learning new ideas and practicing them. This is essential to the goal of completing the pain caused by loss. After working through this book, you will have much better habits for dealing with any losses or disappointments that occur in your life.

WE'RE TAUGHT MYTHS ABOUT
DEALING WITH GRIEF

Before we can discuss what recovery is, it's important to look at what it isn't. We must be clear about why we need to find a new way to deal with loss. We begin by clarifying our understanding of how we have dealt with loss in the past. We will use John's and Russell's experiences with loss as illustrations.

John's first memory about learning to deal with loss comes from when he was five years old:

> *We had a family dog. This dog adopted me from the moment I arrived home from the hospital. When I was old enough to crawl, I'd pull the dog's tail and she'd let me get away with it. The dog would go everywhere with me. As I grew older, I tried to teach the dog to retrieve. (To this day, I'm not sure who taught whom to retrieve.) The dog always found a way to sleep with me each night. This drove my mother to distraction. But the dog and I were persistent and eventually Mom gave up. Then, one morning, I called to my dog and she wouldn't get up. I remember how cold she felt when I touched her. I remember being afraid. I called to my mother to help me. My mother told me that my dog had died. I'm certain she tried to explain what death was. I'm also certain she didn't know how.*

For the next several days after the dog died, John cried a lot and spent a great deal of time in his room. "My parents felt inadequate in knowing what to do to help me," he remembers. Finally, in total frustration, John's father said:

> *Don't cry—on Saturday we'll get you a new dog.*

Now, that doesn't sound like such a profound sentence. But let's take a closer look. We learn by many different methods. One of these is called *influence learning*. A child is born into a family. During the first few years, the child's primary contact is with his or her parents. The child learns from watching and emulating what he sees his parents do. Usually, by eighteen to twenty-four months, the child has gained verbal skills. From this point forward, the child can not only see what his parents are doing but can understand what they say. John's father's words carried the following message:

> *Don't cry . . .*
> **Meaning: Don't feel bad.**

> *. . . on Saturday we'll get you a new dog.*
> **Meaning: Replace the loss.**

John believed his father. He began to form a belief about dealing with loss. He tried to follow his father's advice and not feel bad. To a young child who wanted his father's approval, this was a powerful communication from the most important authority figure in his life. As John explains, "I thought that if this is the way my father deals with death, then this is the way I'm supposed to deal with it."

Sure enough, on Saturday John's dad took him to the kennel and they got a new dog:

> *I still missed my old dog, but I didn't tell anyone. I didn't think they'd approve. After a long period of time, I actually forgot about my old dog. I also found it hard to love the new dog in the same way I'd loved my old dog, and I didn't know why.*

It's possible, in fact likely, that John couldn't love the new dog because he wasn't emotionally complete with the old dog.

When John was fourteen, he fell in love for the first time. It may have been puppy love, but it sure felt like the real thing to him.

> *It was wonderful. I was preoccupied with thoughts of her all the time. I had trouble eating and sleeping. The birds sang. I listened to love songs on the radio. I didn't hang out with my friends as much.*
>
> *When we broke up, I was devastated. This was a major loss for me. For days I wandered around like a wounded duck. Finally, my mother couldn't take it anymore.*

What his mother said was:

> *Don't feel bad—there are plenty of fish in the sea.*

By this point, John had gotten a clear idea about what to do when you lose something. He was going forth into life armed with two pieces of information on dealing with loss:

1. Don't feel bad.
2. Replace the loss.

Russell's childhood experiences were very similar to John's. "Don't feel bad" and "replace the loss" were used in the same kinds of circumstances.

Russell was unable to "not feel bad" when he felt bad. Loss experiences of all kinds made him feel sad. His sadness and tears were often met with comments like, "If you're going to cry, go to your room."

Russell struggled with hiding his feelings. He tried to talk with his mother about still feeling sad. She said to him, "Laugh and the whole world laughs with you, cry and you cry alone." It is heartbreaking to realize that when you are sad and might really benefit from some emotional understanding, you are taught to "be by yourself."

Meaning: Grieve alone.

It would be sad enough if it ended with feeling dismissed and misunderstood as a child. Unfortunately, though, this kind of misinformation becomes the foundation of lifelong habits, many of which directly interfere with our ability to be happy. Russell can remember too many times in his marriages when he stormed out of the house following an argument with his wife and drove aimlessly around the neighborhood. His car became a metaphor for his room as a child. The unchanging habit was to "grieve alone."

Since most of us are socialized in much the way John and Russell were, we usually think that it is correct for us to "isolate" or "grieve alone." Also tragic is the conclusion that stems from what we were taught. If I need to "grieve alone," then you do too. Thus, when a friend has experienced a loss, we often say, "Give her some space," or, "He needs to be alone."

John's experience following the death of his grandfather further illustrates the depth of society's belief in grieving alone.

In 1958 my grandfather died. He was very important in my life. He was probably closer to me than my father was at that point. Every summer was spent at his farm. He taught me how to fish, hunt, and was the first to teach me how to play baseball.

When I was told he'd died, I was sitting in one of my high school classes. I can remember going numb. It was like being in a trance. After several minutes, I began to cry, and I suppose that made everyone uncomfortable. So they sent me to the principal's office so I could be by myself.

Since they didn't know what to do, they sent John to the office to be alone.

Once again, I assumed the adults around me knew what they were doing. This attitude of handling pain alone was further reinforced when I got home that night. My mother was sitting in the living room with her head down and was obviously crying. As soon as I saw her, I wanted to go to her so we could cry together. Both my father and my uncle came and said to me:

"Don't disturb your mother. She'll be okay in a little while."

John and Russell now had three pieces of data on how to deal with loss.

1. Don't feel bad.
2. Replace the loss.
3. Grieve alone.

Not a single one of these lessons was going to be of any help to either of them.

While John was struggling with the death of his grandfather in Illinois, Russell was having a very difficult time as a teenager in Florida.

With each successive loss experience, Russell was constantly met with the same unhelpful ideas. Since he could not find a way to feel better using the ideas he had been taught, his life began to feel smaller and sadder. Each time a painful event occurred, he tried to "not feel bad" and to "grieve alone." He found himself believing that he would never be happy.

Finally, in desperation, he went to his mother. He told her that he could not seem to deal effectively with the thoughts and feelings that were troubling him. She looked at him sweetly and said, "Time heals all wounds."

Meaning: Just give it time.

Russell has absolutely no doubt that his mother loved him. She had no intent to harm her son. She merely passed on to him what had been taught to her.

In 1972 Russell and his first wife Vivienne divorced. Russell was devastated. He walked around like a zombie. Normally talkative and outgoing, he hardly spoke at all. Although he was not supposed to "feel bad," he was crushed. He felt awful. Having been taught to grieve alone, he found himself isolated a lot.

The early training to "replace the loss" was reinforced by well-meaning friends who suggested that he start dating. He didn't feel good, so the idea of dating didn't make sense to him. At the same time, he was being reminded that "time would heal him." The two ideas didn't go together. If replacing the loss was going to fix him, then he didn't have to wait for time to heal him. On the other hand, if time were to heal him, then maybe he shouldn't be in such a hurry to replace the loss.

The concept that time heals is probably responsible for more heartache than any other single wrong idea in our society. The terrible part is, it isn't true. It's one of those false-hoods that's been passed down from generation to generation.

The mistaken idea that after enough time passes something will magically change to make us whole again is preposterous. If we were dealing with any other human pain, no one would say, "Just give it time."

If you came across a person with a broken arm, you would-n't say, "Just give it time." Just as broken bones should be properly set to heal and ultimately function again, so must the *emotional heart*.

We all know too many people whose hearts remain broken partly because they are waiting for time to heal them. Sadly, they come to believe it's true. People wait around for years with the idea that after a long enough period of time they will feel better again. Some of you reading this book already know this isn't true.

In one seminar, we asked people to raise their hands if they were still experiencing pain caused by a death or divorce that occurred more than twenty years ago. As expected, many people indicated this was true for them. They all believed that time would take care of the pain. We asked one woman whether twenty years didn't seem like too long a time to be waiting for recovery. She answered with a clear and classic statement: "Yes, it is, but I don't know what else to do." Can you imagine the pain and frustration? The years of waiting for some relief?

To illustrate the absurdity of waiting for time to heal, we ask this question. If you discovered that your car had a flat tire, would you pull up a chair next to the car and sit and wait for air to some-how get back into the tire? Seems silly, doesn't it?

Time itself does not heal; it is what you *do* within time that will help you complete the pain caused by loss.

Let's recap what John and Russell had learned about grief.

1. Don't feel bad.
2. Replace the loss.
3. Grieve alone.
4. Just give it time.

In 1957 Russell's grandmother died. She had been living with his family since Russell's mom went back to work. Grandma was the primary caretaker for Russell's younger brother, who is ten years younger than Russell. He had never felt particularly close to his grandmother. Sometimes he felt that she was mean to him. In those days in his family, it was not okay to talk negatively about family members—"blood is thicker than water" being the prevailing theme.

When his grandmother died, Russell recalls a family meeting. He remembers being told, "We have to be strong for your brother."

Meaning: Be strong for others.

There were no specific instructions on how to do that. "Be strong for others" is one of those expressions that sounds good but has no real value. Many years later, when Russell and his first wife divorced, his brain came up with, "Be strong for others." This was one of the few ideas Russell had for dealing with grief. In a heartbeat, he realized that this had no application to his divorce and he didn't have a clue what to do because he was the other.

In our twenty-plus years of helping grievers, "be strong" or "be strong for others" makes the top ten list as one of the most confusing of all ideas relating to loss. It is confusing because it is undoable.

At this point, John and Russell had accumulated five pieces of misinformation:

1. Don't feel bad.
2. Replace the loss.
3. Grieve alone.
4. Just give it time.
5. Be strong for others.

There are many ideas that are not helpful for grievers. The five we have listed so far represent those with which you will probably identify. While not absolute, they have a universality to them. This next one is also so common that most people believe it to be true and helpful, yet it is neither.

"You have to keep busy," or, "You must stay active," are two of the clichés that we have all heard following any kind of significant loss.

Meaning: Keep busy.

Here is an important question. Does keeping busy discover and complete the pain caused by loss? The obvious answer is no. Then what does keeping busy accomplish, if anything? It distracts you. It makes one more day go by.

Keeping busy buries the pain of the loss under an avalanche of activity. Every griever we have ever talked to will say, "No matter how busy I stay, at the end of the day, there's still a hole in my heart."

In addition to exhausting you, there are other dangers in keeping busy. Earlier we defined grief as "the conflicting feelings caused by the end of or change in a familiar pattern of behavior." A death, a divorce, or any other major loss produces massive changes in all things familiar. It is very difficult to adapt to life after a loss. If you were never a busy person before a loss, keeping busy would add yet another major change to the familiar.

The most dangerous flaw of keeping busy is the idea that it will make you feel better. Busy-ness is just a distraction. It does not alter the fact that you have to take direct actions to complete the pain caused by loss. We have heard this lament thousands of times: "I don't understand, I kept busy, but I felt worse, not better."

John and Russell and perhaps many of you were sent into life with several pieces of misinformation about dealing with loss. The six we have identified so far are:

1. Don't feel bad.
2. Replace the loss.
3. Grieve alone.
4. Just give it time.
5. Be strong for others.
6. Keep busy.

None of these ideas leads us to the actions of discovering and completing the unfinished emotions that accrue in all relationships.

PARTICIPATING IN YOUR OWN RECOVERY

Earlier we talked about the fact that grievers have been taught to isolate themselves. You have probably experienced such isolation yourself. Since isolation is one of the problems confronting grievers in our society, then participation is clearly part of the solution.

To encourage you to participate in your own recovery, we are going to suggest that you start right now. Using the list of six incorrect ideas as a guide, see if you can think of any other ideas that you were taught or that influenced your beliefs about dealing with sad, painful, or negative feelings.

LOSS OF TRUST

It is normal and natural to feel sad when a sad event happens. But every time we express our normal and natural responses, we are met with one or more of that list of false ideas, starting with, "Don't feel bad."

John and Russell each brought many of their painful emotional experiences to their parents, teachers, coaches, or others, only to be met with intellectual replies. The accumulation of unhelpful reactions began to add up to a loss of trust. While their initial loss-of-trust incident might have been with a parent or other adult authority figure, eventually the blanket of mistrust covered all relationships.

John's father was an alcoholic. When his father was intoxicated, he repeatedly spanked John for things he did not do.

Even though I would tell him it wasn't my fault, he didn't believe me and punished me anyway. It seemed very unfair to me, and my faith in him was diminished.

Since the loss was never acknowledged or settled, John's suspicion of adults expanded. He trusted less and was on guard more. This limited John's aliveness and freedom. It limited the type of people with whom he could have trusting relationships. It caused him to be wary of all authority figures.

"I'm not saying that this general loss of trust was right on my part." Loss of trust was painful, so John learned that the solution was *don't trust*, thereby eliminating the potential for pain.

John's breakup with his first girlfriend reinforced the idea of not trusting people. From that point on, he found he had great difficulty in trusting the girls he dated. He was tentative and held back, since he didn't want to be hurt again. That attitude limited his capacity for aliveness. We know many grievers who have trouble starting up new relationships because they're afraid of enduring another loss. Most of you bought this book because of an awareness that something was not finished in your relationship to a death, a divorce, or another loss. Or you may have been given this book by a well-meaning friend or relative.

As this book unfolds, and as you participate in the actions that lead to recovery, you may recognize a sense of diminished trust. We cannot command you to feel safe or trusting about your feelings. We can, however, suggest that we too have been there. We did not feel safe either. We had been so conditioned to convert our emotions into intellect that we thought we were defective for having feelings at all. Please keep reading, even if you don't trust right now.

PRACTICE MAKES HABITS

Why do we persist in trying to use information that hasn't worked for us? To understand why, you need to know some things about the computer we call the mind.

First, the mind has access only to what it has learned. It cannot use what it doesn't know. If you are given only misinformation, that's all you have access to. Second, the information stored in the mind is stored with importance attached. That means that the more important the source of the information, the more tenaciously we believe it to be right. Most of the data John and Russell acquired about loss came from their parents. To a child, parents are a very important source of information. Third, the mind's job is to believe that whatever it has stored in it is *always right!* This is why people are so critical of each other. If you believe you're right and others don't agree with you, then they must be wrong!

It's for these reasons that we persist in using misinformation in trying to process the feelings caused by loss. We believe that what we already know about loss is right. The fact that you are reading this book implies that what you have practiced is not delivering the relief and sense of well-being you want and deserve.

If you will accept the simple premise that you practiced and habituated some incorrect ideas, then you can allow that if you practice some correct ideas, you will have different results. We will give you correct information to help you discover and complete what is unfinished between you and others, living or dead. You must take action and practice what you learn here.

4

Others Are Ill Prepared to Help Us Deal with Loss

In reading chapter 3, you probably identified with some of the experiences described. You may have recognized some of your own early life experiences in which you learned to process loss incorrectly. Almost everyone in our society has some kind of inadequate and inappropriate information stored in the computer of their mind.

It is only natural and quite healthy for people who are caught in a grieving situation to seek solace from those around them. However, in rather short order it becomes abundantly clear to the griever that friends and associates are not of much help. Even though they are well meaning, they often say things that can seem inappropriate.

THEY DON'T KNOW WHAT TO SAY

Let's start with one of the common phrases heard by griev-ing people. Whether your loss was from death, divorce, or any other major event, you may have heard, "I know how you feel." This is delivered with great compassion, and with intent to soothe.

Most people report that they are anything but soothed by that comment. If the comment is well intended, why do most grievers react strongly against it? The answer lies in the ultimate truth about grief and grief recovery mentioned earlier.

All relationships are unique, no exceptions!

Therefore, no one knows how you feel.

Even a well-meaning friend who has had a parallel loss does not know how you feel. A similar loss is an intellectual fact. It is not emotionally helpful. It does not relate to the uniqueness of the individual relationship. The fact that my mother died and your mother died is nothing more than a shared intellectual fact. This personal fact is not much different or more important than our respective shoe sizes. If this sounds harsh, it is intentional. We must try to stop intellectual connections from overpowering emotional truths.

For example, if you had a warm and fuzzy, supportive relationship with your mom and I had a stormy, combative, painful relationship with my mom, do you "know how I feel?"

Let us repeat:

All relationships are unique, no exceptions!

As you understand and accept this simple premise, you are well on the road to recovery. Recovery means "discovering and completing" what was unfinished for you in your "unique" relationship.

The great majority of well-meaning people around us do not have *successful* grief recovery experiences to share. Therefore, they unwittingly encourage us to *act recovered*. This phenomenon has become so common that our next chapter is devoted to it.

THEY'RE AFRAID OF OUR FEELINGS

Very early on, society teaches us that having sad, painful, or negative feelings and showing them are somehow not appropriate. It starts with the admonition, "Big boys and girls don't cry." One can actually hear parents say, "Stop that crying or I'll give you a reason to cry."

Now, we don't want you to get the idea that parents are insensitive, because that isn't true. They only pass on to their children what they were taught. What they were taught was that sad, painful, or negative feelings and showing them are not acceptable in our society.

"Cry baby, cry baby" can be heard resounding around preschool playgrounds. This is proof that the lesson has already been learned by age four or five.

A small sample of the statements heard on a daily basis illustrates the fear that others have when we show our feelings.

"Get a hold of yourself."
"You can't fall apart."

"Keep a stiff upper lip."
"Pull yourself up by your bootstraps."

As a society, we're uncomfortable when confronted by displays of painful emotion. This all perpetuates a fear of showing the normal feelings that result from emotional loss.

THEY TRY TO CHANGE THE SUBJECT

From time to time, you may have wanted to tell a friend how you were feeling about an important emotional event in your life. You might recall how your friend listened for a while and then said, "That sounds really bad, but have you been watching what's been going on in the stock market?"

This example, while typical, does not explain what is really happening. Let's take another example and look at it closely:

A griever whose mother has died tries to communicate with a friend.

FRIEND: How are you doing?
GRIEVER: I'm heartbroken. I miss her so much.
FRIEND: Don't feel bad, she's not in pain anymore.

Look at this subtle change of subject. It is the griever who is sad, and the friend shifts to talking about the person who died. The implication is that if your loved one is no longer suffering, then you shouldn't be either.

We should note that the skills and tools used by the friend in this scenario are no better or worse than those of most people in our society. The friend has been socialized with the same false ideas that we all learned. The friend is lovingly trying to execute the training received over a lifetime.

This change-the-subject attitude was displayed on the ABC television program *20/20* in a show about grief caused by the death of a pet. The program was really well done and very sensitive to a griever's feelings. When the segment was over, the camera shifted back to Hugh Downs and Barbara Walters. Walters had started to get tears in her eyes. Her final remark before the commercial was, "Before I cry, let's change the subject."

The clear message to viewers was that showing feelings is not acceptable. In other words, "Let's deal with our feelings by changing the subject."

THEY INTELLECTUALIZE

The attempt to shift from emotions to intellect is a dangerous and counterproductive thing to do with grieving people. Grief is, by definition, the emotional response to loss. The cause of the loss itself is intellectual, but the reaction to it is emotional.

That's not to say there is anything wrong with using our minds, but where is it written that we can't employ both intellect and emotions when they're called for? One of humanity's great gifts is the ability to demonstrate and communicate emotions. Yet society seems to place negative value on this gift.

Our reliance on intellect at the expense of feelings has reached epidemic proportions—particularly where grief is concerned. One reason is that the death of a loved one is not an everyday occurrence. If statistics are to be believed, we will each experience the death of a loved one every nine to thirteen years. Even when combined with other significant emotional losses, a major grief event occurs so infrequently that we never really get familiar with the experience. Because of our lack of personal knowledge, we continue the habit of dealing with loss based on misinformation. This habit leads to the unsuccessful conclusion of grief events. It is not surprising that people approach emotional pain intellectually. Since we rely on our minds every day, we're far more practiced at using them.

Based on the informal surveys we conduct at each of our seminars, an average of four out of five reactions that grievers hear following the loss of a loved one imply that they shouldn't deal with the feelings they are experiencing. The things they hear usually appeal to the intellect. Researchers have studied the statements typically heard by grievers very shortly after a death. Many of these comments are so common that they have been identified and can be divided into two categories: (1) those that are helpful to grievers and (2) those that are not. The unhelpful comments are all well-meaning but invariably appeal to the intellect or give advice that is difficult or dangerous to follow, such as:

> "Be thankful you have another son."
> "The living must go on."
> "He's in a better place."
> "All things must pass."
> "She led a full life."
> "You'll find somebody else."
> "God will never give you more than you can handle."
> "Be grateful you had him for so long."

These are all comments that we ourselves as grievers have heard. Since the griever is experiencing intense emotional suffering, these statements, which all have to do with the intellect, are quite inappropriate. Divorce and other significant emotional losses generate similar unhelpful comments from well-meaning friends.

THEY DON'T HEAR US

Let's not limit the discussion to the comments heard following a death or divorce. The following situation, which has nothing to do with death or divorce, illustrates how incorrectly others often respond to our normal feelings. One of our friends was having a party. Her teenage daughter, Mary, had invited three of her best friends to the event. As the party was starting, the phone rang several times. The three best friends each called to say they had made other plans. Mary was very upset. She went to her mom and told her what had happened. Mom said, "Don't feel bad, there are a lot of nice people here to enjoy." Do you remember that when John's dog died, and when his grandpa died, the first response was always, "Don't feel bad." Here we go again—don't feel the way you feel, because sad, painful, or negative feelings are no good. You must find a more acceptable feeling, something positive.

Fortunately, a close friend of the family was standing nearby. Mary decided to take another chance at getting someone to hear what she was saying. She told the friend what had happened. He listened and then responded: "Ouch, you must be *so* disappointed." "Yes," she sobbed. He hugged her. She thanked him for listening, went and cleaned up her face, and then enjoyed the party, *after* her feelings were heard and acknowledged.

Grieving people want and need to be *heard*, not fixed. In this true story, the family friend didn't repair anything; he merely heard the emotion being communicated. That was all

Mary needed. She could then make the intellectual decision to enjoy the balance of the evening even though it was not going to be exactly as she had envisioned it. To a certain degree, effective grief recovery is about being heard.

THEY DON'T WANT TO TALK ABOUT DEATH

Another form of distraction is how people talk, or don't talk, about death. In fact, we've gone to such extremes to avoid talk about death that some of us can't even say the word *death*. Think about it:

> "She passed away."
> "He's gone to his eternal rest."
> "Dad's gone."
> "He expired."
> "We've lost Mother."

Imagine how all this sounds to small children, who expect to hear truthful answers.

> *What happened to Grandpa?*
> *Grandpa's gone to sleep.*

The child takes one look at Grandpa in the casket and knows something isn't quite right about that answer. He's confused but assumes he's been told the truth. There must be two types of sleep. So he then spends the next six months being afraid to go to sleep at night.

We're sorry to say this, but God has been given a bad name where children are concerned.

What happened to my daddy?
God has called him home.

For the next several years, the child is upset and confused by God. Don't you think it might be more appropriate to tell the child what the parents believe to be the truth? "Your dad has died. And we believe that after he died, he went to be with God."

Generally, it is best to avoid all metaphors when speaking about death with children. Developing young minds do not always have the ability to match reality with metaphorical images.

PROFESSIONAL DISTORTIONS

Our beliefs establish how we feel. If we have false ideas, we are liable to generate false feelings. The particular area that seems to have been the most shrouded in incorrect ideas is grief, so much so that the word *grief* is often replaced by inaccurate and confusing words.

When a loss occurs, a person experiences grief. Grief is the entire range of naturally occurring human emotions that accompany loss. When grief is incorrectly defined, a griever is unwittingly discouraged from following the normal sequence of emotions and actions that could lead to recovery. Grief is the normal and natural reaction to loss. Of itself, it is neither a pathological condition nor a personality disorder. Pressure, burnout, stress, PTSD (post-traumatic stress disorder), or

ADD (attention deficit disorder) are some of the false labels applied to grief. Those words have meaning and value when used in their correct context. But they become dangerous and misleading when misused.

Perhaps the most misused and misunderstood word on the topic of grief is *depression.* Tragically, it is the incorrect use of this one word that has engendered an epidemic of pharmacological intervention in grief.

We want this book to be helpful, without reading like a textbook. To keep this as simple as possible, let us give you an idea of what we mean. Clinical depression, as defined by a psychiatrist or psychologist, includes many of the same symptoms that a grieving person might report following a death or divorce. When grievers use the word *depression,* they typically are signifying "a lowered state of feeling or energy." Let's say someone's spouse of forty years has died. Doesn't a lowered level of energy seem logical? Isn't the griever entitled to some diminished feelings as he or she adapts to the painful and confusing new reality? We think so.

Many people have been conditioned to seek a medical solution to a nonmedical problem. This can be dangerous. Treatment of grief in the form of psychotropic drugs can hide the normal and natural reactions to loss. Once buried, it is difficult to reconnect those feelings at a later date.

From a grief recovery perspective, drug therapies fall into the general category of short-term energy-relieving behaviors (STERBs). There is no doubt that drugs have the capacity to divert and distract. In certain circumstances, an individual can derive some short-term benefit from the use of low-dosage mind-altering drugs. The danger is in the illusion of well-being that often accompanies such treatment. This illusion may lead to long-term dependence on the drugs.

You may feel substantial pressure from professionals and family members to begin drug treatment in response to loss. Try to remember that they too were socialized in the same world that taught us to respond to feelings with substances. "Don't feel bad, have some milk and cookies, you'll feel better." Be alert to the parallel idea, "Don't feel bad, have a pill, you'll feel better."

We know that during this vulnerable time you may have difficulty making reasoned decisions. We suggest that you try to accept the naturally occurring pain caused by your loss and attempt the program of recovery outlined in this book. If you find it too difficult, you can always use the drugs as a second alternative.

We are not promoting pain. If there were a softer, easier way, we would tell you about it. Grief is painful. It is supposed to be. Our experience shows clearly that approaching grief naturally has much more long-term benefit than any other option.

THEY WANT US TO KEEP OUR FAITH

In 1969 John's younger brother died. John remembers being told, "You shouldn't be angry with God."

John knew he shouldn't be angry with God, but he was anyway. No one knew to tell him that anger at God is a typical response to an untimely death. We've relied on intellect for years, so we search for understandable reasons for events. When we can't find a reason, we assign blame to God.

This anger will pass if we're allowed to express the feeling. We have to be allowed to tell someone that we're angry with God and not be judged for it, or told that we're bad because of it. If not, this anger may persist forever and block spiritual growth. We've known people who never returned to their religion because they weren't allowed to express their true feelings. If this happens, the griever is cut off from one of the most powerful sources of support he or she might have.

Faith and Feelings: There Is a Difference

Over the past several years, we have found it helpful to ask grievers to distinguish between faith and feelings. We realize that may sound like a strange idea, but most people sense what we mean by it. We have been discussing emotions and intellect. Now we need to address the spiritual aspect of grief. While it may be possible to find a direct cause-and-effect linkage between intellectual thoughts and the feelings that follow, faith is different. Faith does not require reason. It is spiritual, not emotional or intellectual.

There are two very distinct probabilities following a loss: (1) your religious or spiritual faith may be shattered or shaken, or (2) regardless of the nature of the loss, your faith is undamaged.

It is most often the death of a child or a sudden tragic accident that creates a major breach in a person's faith. We suggest that the griever work first on his or her relationship with the person who died. After completing the pain caused by that loss, faith usually returns naturally, and often with renewed intensity. If faith does not return, we help people heal their loss of trust in God. We use the same principles to complete loss-of-trust experiences with parents, doctors, clergy, and therapists.

For those whose faith is not damaged, we encourage them to use the power of their faith to give them the courage to take the actions of grief recovery. Again, to use the metaphor of the flat tire, here are two choices: (1) to sit down in front of the flat tire and pray for God to cause air to get back in, or (2) to call the automobile club, then pray to God to have the auto club get there quickly.

Unresolved grief is always about undelivered emotional communications that accrue within a relationship over the course of time. Faith and prayer are wonderful tools to apply to daily living. However, faith and prayer do not, of themselves, discover and complete what is unfinished.

In religious terms, it is said that God helps those who help themselves. We agree. We believe that helping ourselves is taking the actions of grief recovery—discovering and completing what is unfinished for us in our relationships.

5

Academy Award Recovery

In the last chapter, we mentioned the fact that society literally teaches us to *act recovered*. Understanding this aspect of grief is enormously important. A false image of recovery is the most common obstacle all grievers must overcome if they expect to move beyond their loss. *Academy award recovery* is its name. It could also be called "I'm fine," or, "Put on your happy face," or, "Be fine for my family and friends," or, "I want to help others." You might sit down and ask yourself how many of these "act-recovered" faces you're currently using. Most of you already know what we're talking about.

In the previous chapter, we discussed how those around the griever respond at the time of a loss. We showed that the vast majority of comments a griever hears appeal to the intellect and do not encourage the expression of feelings. Such intellectualizing increases a griever's sense of isolation and creates a feeling of being judged, evaluated, and criticized. In a relatively short time, the griever discovers that he or she must indeed "act recovered" in order to be treated in an acceptable manner.

ENSHRINE OR BEDEVIL?

In an attempt to be accepted and to look recovered, grievers try to focus on only fond memories. Where incomplete grief is concerned, this is known as "enshrinement." Enshrinement, in its most damaging form, can include obsessively building memorials to the person who died. This can be demonstrated by keeping large numbers of objects that represent the person. An example is the mother who did not change one item in her daughter's room although her daughter had been dead for more than five years.

Less critical but equally limiting is the enshrinement that simply doesn't allow the griever to look accurately at all aspects of the relationship. Many grievers limit their thoughts and feelings to fond memories or positive comments about the deceased. The idea that "you must not speak ill of the dead" is an example of unhelpful information. We do not suggest that anyone run around badmouthing anybody, living or dead. We do suggest that it's almost impossible to complete the pain caused by death, divorce, or other significant emotional loss without looking at everything about the relationship, not just the positive.

Bedevilment is the opposite of enshrinement. The griever has a litany of complaints detailing a lifetime of mistreatment. They are unwilling to let go of disappointments and anger. With bedevilment, the griever clings to the negatives just as the enshriner clings to the positives, but neither views the entire relationship.

All relationships include both positive and negative interactions. We know that you can complete grief only by being totally honest with yourself and others.

WE WANT THE APPROVAL OF OTHERS

We all like praise and compliments. We all like approval. We all want to be seen as smart, strong, and mature. We all want to feel as if we are part of the group. This need is learned during early childhood and often reinforced to the point of obsession.

Earlier we mentioned that a large percentage of the comments made to grieving people following a loss are not helpful. Grievers are advised to take actions that merely distract or to convert feelings into intellectual ideas. Since approval is such a powerful aspect of our social skills, we try to conform to the ideas suggested to us following a loss.

When John's infant son died, it tore him apart. What he heard, however, were comments such as:

> "You and your wife should be grateful that you can have other children."
> "It was just not meant to be."
> "You're strong enough to handle it."

While intellectually all these statements were true, they still didn't help John to deal with his feelings. John sensed that his friends didn't want to hear about his feelings. But he didn't want to be alone. The question was, how could he honestly share his feelings without driving listeners away?

When Russell and his first wife divorced, well-meaning friends said:

> "You'll do better next time."
> "She wasn't right for you."

Russell had a normal need to be heard. But those comments stopped him from talking and inadvertently encouraged him to bury his feelings.

John and Russell both wanted the approval of those around them. They were tired of feeling bad, but they did not feel supported by their family and friends in their attempts to feel better. So they opted for academy award recovery. They began to put on their academy award faces even though they were not recovered by any stretch of the imagination. Their performances were so good that they nearly convinced themselves that they were all right when they were not.

"I'M FINE" IS OFTEN A LIE

Through our work with grievers around the country, we get to see some of the most put-together people on earth. They look good, they sound good, and they even try to convince us they are feeling good. When we meet people who've just experienced a loss, we ask them how they're doing. Invariably, the answer is the same: "I'm fine."

When we make speeches to large groups, we often ask how many people like being lied to. Of course, no one raises their hand. Then we ask how many of them have lied about their feelings following sad or painful events. All of the hands go up. It is very sad when you realize that we have been taught to lie about our feelings for fear of being judged or criticized.

The danger of "I'm fine" is that it does not help the broken heart. Saying "I'm fine" merely distracts us and others, while pain and loneliness persist on the inside. The net effect is to create a scab over an infection, leaving a mess underneath.

WE BEGIN TO EXPERIENCE A MASSIVE LOSS OF ENERGY

In talking with thousands and thousands of grievers, we have rarely had a griever argue with us when we say that it sounds like they just don't have any energy left. Sometimes it is all a griever can do to get out of bed and go through the motions of a day, a week, a month, and eventually a lifetime on automatic pilot, with almost no energy.

Unresolved grief consumes tremendous amounts of energy. Most commonly, the grief stays buried under the surface, and *only the symptoms are treated*. Many people, including mental health professionals, misunderstand the fact that *unresolved loss is cumulative and cumulatively negative*.

It is reasonable to suggest that human energy is used most efficiently when our minds and bodies are in harmony. Unresolved grief tends to separate us from ourselves. As an example, how many times have you been driving down the road and then suddenly realized that for the last three blocks you were anywhere but driving the car? You were in your head, having a conversation with someone who was not in the car. And it's a miracle that you're still alive. Quite often those phantom conversations are with someone who has died or with a former spouse. More likely than not, these conversations represent an aspect of unfinished emotional business between you and someone else, living or dead. Holding on to incomplete emotions consumes enormous amounts of energy.

WE EXPERIENCE A LOSS OF ALIVENESS

As a direct result of living in the deception of academy award recovery, many people experience a kind of false recovery based on their convincing performance. This can lead to a loss of aliveness and spontaneity that is almost impossible to overcome. Many people fall into a trap of quiet desperation—sometimes feeling good, sometimes feeling bad, but never being able to return to a state of full happiness and joy.

We pay a high price for the incorrect information we have about dealing with loss. Each time a loss is not properly concluded, there is cumulative restriction on our aliveness. Life becomes something to endure; the world seems like a hostile place in which to live. Because of misinformation, we never had a fair chance to deal effectively with the loss events in our lives.

Some of you are reading this book for reasons other than death or divorce. You might reflect upon your childhood; life was going to be happy and joyous. But owing to many small but unresolved losses over time, you may have awakened one day to find that life had just not worked out the way you hoped it would.

Some of you may not even remember having the idea that life was going to be wonderful. For you, there may be a cumulative sense that your life is not happy—but discontent is all you know. You may have very little or no reference point for joy.

In either case, you may have tried in many ways to improve your sense of happiness and well-being. Therapy, religious or spiritual beliefs, or twelve-step programs may have contributed valuable insights and tools. And yet, you may have a lingering sense that you are incomplete with your past, a feeling that, in turn, diminishes your hopes about the future.

Please do not stop now. This book is for you too.

PART TWO

Preparing for Change: Starting to Recover

Recovery from loss is achieved by a series of small and correct choices made by the griever. You have already made several correct choices:

> You have acknowledged that a problem exists.
> You have acknowledged that the problem is associated with loss.
> You have acknowledged, by beginning to read this handbook, that you are now willing to take action to complete your grief.

The next four chapters will introduce you to the first actions necessary for moving beyond loss. Success in moving through grief depends on your willingness to follow through on each action along the way.

6

Your First Choice: Choosing to Recover

To make the choice to recover, we need to know where and how to begin. There are three words that help us begin the process of recovery: *different, better, or more.*

Whether the loss is a death, a divorce, or a painful estrangement from another person, the question "What do you wish had been *different, better, or more?*" will always help you find what is incomplete.

Let's go back to John's story from the day his grandfather died.

When John was sent to the principal's office to be alone, it reinforced the lesson he'd been taught all of his life about not talking about his feelings. As John sat in the office and reflected on the relationship, he wanted to thank his grandfather for all he had learned from him. John had often put off expressing his feelings until a later date. Before "later" arrived, his grandfather died. John was stuck with the undelivered "thank you." This was one of the things he wished had been *different, better, or more.*

John started to feel bad about the choices he had made. Many people in our world mistakenly call this guilt. Wishing that things could somehow have been **different, better, or more** is not the same as feeling guilty.

If we do not identify *different, better, or more,* we begin to make the death or other loss responsible for how bad we feel. As long as we believe that someone or something else is responsible, we're unable to recover.

WHO IS RESPONSIBLE?

After recognizing the fallacy that "grief just takes time," the next most difficult hurdle for grievers to overcome is the incorrect belief that other people or events are responsible for their feelings. Many have a tendency to say:

> "So-and-so made me angry."
> "So-and-so ruined my day."
> "I'd be okay if So-and-so hadn't done such-and-such to me."

This attitude of nonresponsibility for our feelings and our actions is rampant. This too starts with early "influence learning."

> Mom says to the child, "You make me happy."
> Dad says, "You make me proud."
> Mom says, "Don't make your daddy mad."

As the direct result of being told that their actions cause feelings in Mom or Dad, children realize that the opposite must also be true. *If I can make Mom or Dad feel something, then they can make me feel something.* This is a major contribution to the "victim" mentality that has crept into so many areas of modern life.

To paraphrase Eleanor Roosevelt, *no one can make you feel bad about yourself without your permission.* But even with the help of that very accurate statement, we find it increasingly difficult to dissuade people from the belief that others are responsible for their feelings. When we make other people or events 100 percent responsible for causing our feelings, then we also make them responsible for ending our feelings.

There's a story we've often used to illustrate this concept. We call it the "on the way to work in the car" story.

> *One morning a man is on his way to work in his car. He comes to a red light, and being a law-abiding person, he stops. Sitting at the light, he begins to daydream. Meanwhile, the light changes from red to green. Our friend doesn't see the light change; the driver in the car behind him does. When our friend's car doesn't move, the guy behind him sounds his horn to notify him that the light has turned green. Our friend then rolls down his window and thanks the guy behind him for honking at him and calling his attention to the fact that the light has changed.*

Whom are we kidding here? We all know that it goes more like this.

> *Our friend becomes embarrassed. No one likes to feel embarrassed. He sure doesn't want to be responsible for causing his own embarrassment. He too has a lifetime's practice of making others responsible for his feelings. So, instead of saying "Thank*

*you" to the driver for calling his attention to the fact that the
light has changed, he thinks: "Boy, that guy makes me mad!"*

Almost at once, his mind becomes filled with plans and
schemes to save face or get even. He rolls down his window,
puts his head out, and does exactly what he learned to do in
that self-help seminar he attended two years before. He
reports his feelings: "Hey, buddy, get off my back!"

*He then proceeds to drive a little bit slower in front of this
guy in order to punish him for ruining his day. He knows he's
right about this one!*

Our friend is angry and cannot see that he is the architect
of his own discomfort. He doesn't acknowledge that he is
indeed responsible for the feelings that result from his attitudes and actions.

What ruins the picnic—the rain or one's attitude about
the rain? This is a trick question. The answer is both. The
rain really does ruin the picnic, but you cannot do anything
about the rain, you can only deal with your reaction to the
rain. The same is true of almost all losses. What causes my
grief—the loss or my reaction to the loss? Again, the answer
is both. While we cannot undo what has happened, we can
do something about our reaction. We can acquire skills to
help us complete our relationship to the pain, disappointment, frustration, and heartache caused by what has happened.

Some people are ready to believe that a late bus or a serving
of cold eggs is the result of an international conspiracy. Others
think that the government is ruining their lives, or that the
boss is the cause of their misery. But what this all boils down

to is the belief that "they make me angry." This leads to an almost automatic critical response toward anyone or anything we misperceive as being responsible for our feelings. We become expert at *other*-examination rather than *self*-examination.

As children, we could not change the actions of parents and other adults. Sometime after our childhood, we may become aware of events that happened before we had the power to alter them. We must take responsibility for our *current reaction* to what happened in the past. Otherwise, we will forever feel like a victim.

It is bad enough that horrible things happened to us. It becomes diabolical when we ourselves sustain and re-create the pain through our own memories. The problem is heightened by the fact that we were not taught correct skills to complete the pain caused by the memories of long-ago events.

We have been falsely socialized to believe that we are victims of events and helpless in our responses to those events, as well as to the thoughts, feelings, and actions of others. Therefore, we inevitably believe that the rain is exclusively responsible for our disappointment. Most people are advised to just "let it go" or told that "what's done is done." It would be ideal if the human brain and human heart could simply dismiss problems and move on. But it does not work that way. Nothing can change until you take responsibility for your own recovery. To assist you in breaking the habit of feeling 100 percent a victim of a loss, we are going to ask you to adopt a new idea. We ask you to take 1 percent responsibility for your part of what is incomplete. Inasmuch as a small key can unlock a large door, 1 percent responsibility can open your head and your heart to the path of recovery. For now, that means continuing to turn the pages so you can find the solution.

YOUR SECOND CHOICE: PARTNERSHIP OR WORKING ALONE

In a perfect world, the process of grief recovery would occur in a group setting. The stimulus of many people's stories helps others create accurate memory pictures of their own losses. If you are reading this book, it may be because you have no direct access to one of our Grief Recovery Seminars or Grief Recovery Outreach Programs.

In the first edition of *The Grief Recovery Handbook*, readers were told that recovery from loss could not be achieved alone, that they had to have a partner. Sadly, many people saw that and put the book down. As a result, they did not take the actions that lead to recovery from significant emotional loss. Since that time, we have discovered that recovery is always possible, even if you're working alone.

For Those Working Alone

If circumstances and events in your life make it unrealistic or too fearful for you to have a partner, then *take the actions in this book alone*. Don't stop now.

We will present the applicable instructions for your grief recovery actions whether you are working with or without a partner.

Partners

We still believe that, *if you have a choice*, it is best to have a partner, someone who is working on their own loss. As a rule, they would be working on a different loss than you. However, following a death, it is not uncommon for family members to be partners. They might even work on the same loss. But since every relationship is unique, the recovery will also be unique. It is also perfectly okay within a partnership if one person is working on a death and the other on a divorce or some other loss.

FINDING A PARTNER

You may feel that no one really understands the pain you're in. You may feel that even your own friends don't really comprehend your sorrow. When people say they understand, they really can't. They didn't have the same relationship that you had. Even other family members had their own special relationships.

Grievers are often told to seek others who have experienced a similar loss. Widows are told they can relate only to widows; parents who have lost children are told they can relate only to other such parents. This is false. We have found that anyone who has suffered intense emotional loss can become an ideal partner.

It may be that another family member is grieving over the same death. If you haven't clearly expressed how you're feeling, he or she may not know. You may already have a built-in partner for your recovery work in your own family.

If not, there are countless places to look for such a new friend. At work, you've heard people talk about someone who died. Your local health club, the grocery store, and your religious or social organization are all places where you can find another griever. Bring up the topic of grief at a social gathering. Everyone has a story. They may be thrilled to discover that a program of recovery is available.

When you do find potential partners, be honest with them. Show them this book and tell them what you plan to do. Ask whether they're tired of hurting too. See whether they're willing to recover with you. Don't be discouraged if several choose not to. You'll hear all kinds of excuses. Just keep looking until you're successful.

7

Setting the Guidelines

In this chapter, we presume that you have either found a partner or chosen to work alone. Here are the specific guidelines for the initial partner meeting. *Even if you are working alone, read this part.* Some of the commitments and instructions, as noted, are also for you.

INITIAL PARTNERS MEETING

Your first meeting will not require a great deal of time. An hour should be enough. There will be five more meetings to process the actions outlined in this book. You will probably need at least two or three days between meetings to complete reading and homework assignments.

At this first meeting, establish which day or night works best for both of you. You will probably want to allow at least an hour and a half or two hours for all subsequent meetings.

Make sure you *always* choose a place that will be safe.

Talking about your losses will probably generate some normal and natural human emotions, which may be accompanied by tears. Crying is normal and natural, especially in response to thoughts or discussions about grief. But crying is not essential. Do not decide that you or your partner are defective if there are no tears. By the same token, do not put a false value on tears. Crying is not completion. One of you make a commitment to supply tissues.

Establish within your partnership whether hugs are safe for both of you. Some people do not wish to be hugged. Let that be okay. Also, as a rule, do not hug or touch your partner in the middle of an exercise. Wait until the end. Often physical touch stops a feeling that might otherwise be helpful.

In general, we suggest that you sit a reasonable distance apart, so that the person talking does not feel smothered or intimidated. Try to think of yourselves as friends having a conversation. *This is not therapy.* The topic may seem awkward at first, but the goal is to feel comfortable and safe talking about loss. We suggest that you think of yourself as a *heart with ears* as you listen to your partner.

MAKING COMMITMENTS

You must make certain commitments if the grief recovery process is to work for you.

1: *Total Honesty* (for both partners and those working alone). When we say total honesty, we mean that you should be honest to the best of your ability about the loss events in your life and your feelings about them. Your ability to see and therefore tell the truth about these things will improve as you continue to work in this program. Total honesty means telling the truth *about yourself,* not about anyone else. Don't slip into the trap of talking about someone else. You can tell the truth only about yourself. When it comes to others, you are only guessing.

In no way are we assuming that you, the reader, are a dishonest person. There may be some things that you would be unwilling to tell to a partner. The facts and details about certain events may be too difficult to expose. That's okay. It is more important that you tell the truth about your emotional response to the events. Of course, those of you working alone need to be absolutely honest with yourselves.

2: *Absolute Confidentiality* (for partners). During the course of the work you must do, you're going to talk about emotionally painful events and circumstances in your life. Absolute confidentiality means that you carry any personal information shared by your partner to the grave with you. Absolute confidentiality means you trust your partner to do the same. It means that you must never breach your partner's confidence.

3: *Uniqueness and Individuality* (for partners and those working alone). The third commitment is to the uniqueness and individuality of each person's recovery. Since every relationship is unique, each set of recovery communications is unique. And since every griever brings a unique set of beliefs to the process of recovery, it is essential that you not compare beliefs. Comparison often leads to minimizing or maximizing, not to the truth. No one's opinion about your grief or beliefs is important other than your own. The safety of your partnership and your individual recovery hinges on each of you being able to communicate your own thoughts and feelings without interruption, analysis, criticism, or judgment.

Whether working alone or with a partner, it is essential that you support your recovery with commitments to take the actions of this program seriously, and to do all of the assignments in a timely manner.

Partners: Make sure that you verbalize and acknowledge these commitments to each other.

Those Working Alone: You are only required to make the first commitment. However, it is especially important that you take it seriously. You are also advised to look at the third commitment, particularly the part about not being judgmental or critical of yourself.

FIRST HOMEWORK ASSIGNMENT

Both partners and those working alone should read or reread the first six chapters of this handbook. Make notes and underline statements that affect you. Note things that you relate to from your own experience.

Here is the list of myths John and Russell had learned in dealing with the losses in their lives:

1. Don't feel bad.
2. Replace the loss.
3. Grieve alone.
4. Just give it time.

5. Be strong for others.
6. Keep busy.

Don't be surprised if you relate to most or all of them. It is very common in our society to have been socialized with exactly these beliefs.

Using a clean sheet of paper, write down any of the six ideas to which you relate. Add any other ideas that you were taught or have observed in those around you in connection with loss events. This list will begin to personalize your recovery.

Next, review the following list of clichés. See how many of the comments you have heard and learned to believe. Again, don't be surprised if most or all of them sound familiar. These beliefs about grief are very common in our society. Add any other comments you may have heard in connection with loss events.

"Get a hold of yourself."
"You can't fall apart."
"Keep a stiff upper lip."
"Pull yourself up by your bootstraps."
"We understand how you feel."
"Be thankful you have other children."
"The living must go on."
"He's in a better place."
"All things must pass."
"She led a full life."
"God will never give you more than you can handle."
"You shouldn't be angry with God."

This list represents many of the concepts, beliefs, and ideas that you have been trying to use in dealing with the losses in your life.

Even though this list seems long, we've rarely met anyone who could not add several variations to it. Please do not perceive this as a criticism of you, your family, your church, or society in general. It is essential that you identify which ideas you are using to deal with grief so that you can see whether they are helping or hindering your recovery. Be thorough. The more truth you put into this exercise, the easier it will be for you to adapt to some better ideas of recovery later in this book.

REVIEW THOUGHTS AND REMINDERS

Earlier we noted some false ideas that limit our ability to deal effectively with grief, including:

"Get a hold of yourself."
"You can't fall apart."
"Keep a stiff upper lip."
"Pull yourself up by your bootstraps."

We must always remind ourselves that grief is the *normal and natural* response to loss. Grief is a human response that lets us know that for the moment things are different than they were before the loss. These four comments imply that there is something *wrong* or *defective* about us when we react normally to loss events. Yet it is normal to be overwhelmed when an overwhelming event or series of events occurs. It is normal to feel lost, dazed, confused, and frustrated when major losses affect our lives. It is common to hear that someone, in response to the emotion or as a reaction to loss, *broke down* or *lost it*. It is tragic that such incorrect language and ideas have poisoned our beliefs about dealing with the normal and healthy feelings associated with loss.

SECOND PARTNERS MEETING

Begin by reaffirming your commitments to total honesty, absolute confidentiality, and the uniqueness of your individual recovery. As always, meet in a private place where you will not feel uncomfortable if you cry. Have tissues handy.

This meeting is your first real opportunity to determine what ideas you have been using to deal with all of the losses in your life. This meeting is the only one in which you will have a chance to talk in a general way about grief and loss and to discuss the things you have been led to believe. Later meetings will be more specific as you move toward completion.

There are three potential pitfalls. The first is a tendency to monologue rather than discuss. The second is to become analytical, critical, or judgmental. The third is to bring in ideas from religious, spiritual, intellectual, therapeutic, or twelve-step philosophies. While all of those arenas have substantial value in day-to-day living, their ideas are often confusing when applied to grief.

The objectives are to establish that each of you has substantial misinformation about dealing with loss and to create safety between you. Safety will help reduce isolation and increase participation. You may be surprised to see how much you have in common.

Each of you, in turn, will read your list of myths. These will be some or all of the six myths that John and Russell learned early in their lives. Spend some time discussing the impact those myths had on your life.

Then, taking turns, read your list of other ideas that illustrate the concepts and beliefs you have been using to deal with loss. Again, spend some time discussing the impact those myths have had on your life.

Make plans for your next meeting.

For Those Working Alone

Set aside some time to reread the first six chapters. Review the lists you made and compare them with those in the book. Think about the impact they have had on your life and then jot down notes about that impact. Ask yourself this awkward question: "Am I working alone in part because of some of the beliefs I learned about dealing with painful feelings?"

8

Identifying Short-Term
Energy Relievers

The death of a loved one, divorce, and all other losses produce an incredible amount of emotional energy. Since we have all been socialized from early on to deal with sad, painful, and negative emotions incorrectly, we end up storing the energy inside ourselves.

The most clichéd of stories illustrates that fact. A little child comes home from preschool with her feelings hurt by interactions with the other children on the playground. Mom, Dad, Grandma, or any other caretaker says, "What happened?" The child responds, tearfully, that one of the kids was mean to her. The caretaker says, "Don't cry, here, have a cookie, you'll feel better," thus setting the child up with a life-time belief, from an important authority source, that *feelings can be fixed with food.*

Upon eating the cookie, the child feels *different*, not better, and for the moment is distracted and forgets about the incident on the playground. However, there has been no completion of the emotional pain caused by the event. The event and the feelings attached to it are now buried under the cookie, the sugar, and the distraction. If the child were to bring it up sometime later, she would probably be told, "We don't cry over spilled milk," as if to say that it is not okay to continue having feelings about the incident. So it must stay buried.

Early on we learn to cover up, hide, or bury our feelings under food. It is not surprising that sometime later we adapt that same behavior and cover up our feelings under alcohol or other drugs. We may have learned to do so by observing family members at funerals or wakes consuming large amounts of food and alcohol. Consuming food or alcohol in response to the emotional energy created by death or divorce does not help us discover the source of the energy or complete the relationship affected by our loss. Therefore, we are participating in an *illusion* that the short-term relief offered by food or alcohol gives us long-term relief from the pain caused by the loss.

Food and alcohol are obvious and typical short-term energy-relieving behaviors. There are many, many other short-term behaviors that have the same life-limiting and damaging consequences. Here is a partial list of behaviors that, if done for the wrong reasons, can have a negative impact on grieving people:

- Food
- Alcohol/Drugs
- Anger
- Exercise
- Fantasy (movies, TV, books)
- Isolation
- Sex
- Shopping (humorously called retail therapy)
- Workaholism

Most of these actions are not harmful in and of themselves. They become harmful when you engage in them for the wrong reasons. Just as eating a cookie does not help the emotional pain of loss, shopping provides no long-term help for the pain caused by death or divorce. In fact, it can have quite the opposite effect: the shopping binge is often followed by remorse over the wasted money. This is a further distraction from the real and original emotional event—the death, divorce, or other loss.

While many short-term energy relievers are apparent, some are not. The following example illustrates another, more subtle danger.

It's not uncommon for people to visit grave sites on an extremely regular basis for years following a death. They feel as if the death robbed them of the chance to complete their emotional relationship, and so they often visit the place that best helps them feel close to their loved one. Unconsciously, these grievers are seeking some relief from the pain caused by the incomplete relationship. The problem is that visiting the grave doesn't lead to permanent relief or completion with the person who died.

At the end of this chapter, you will have an opportunity to look at how certain actions of your own may have been indirect ways of dealing with the feelings caused by loss.

SHORT-TERM RELIEF DOESN'T WORK

Imagine a steam kettle filled with water. The flame under the kettle is turned up high. Normally, as the water heats and boils, the steam generated by the heat releases through the spout. Most kettles are fitted with a whistle to notify us when the water has reached the boiling point. Imagine that same steam kettle filled with water, with a high flame burning below and a cork jammed into the spout. Imagine the pressure that builds up inside that kettle when the spout cannot release the built-up energy. The cork represents a lifetime of misinformation that causes us to believe that we are not supposed to talk about sad, painful, or negative emotions.

A healthy steam kettle releases energy immediately as it builds up. When you are told, "Don't feel bad," and, "If you're going to cry, go to your room," the energy stays inside you. The myth that "time will heal" is laughable in terms of the steam kettle analogy. Time only moves the steam kettle closer to an explosion.

As the pressure builds up inside our personal steam kettle, we automatically seek relief. This is when we may start participating in the short-term energy relieving behaviors (STERBs) referred to in chapter 4. There are three major problems with STERBs. The first is that they work, or more accurately, they *appear* to work. They create an illusion of recovery by causing you to forget or bury emotions. The second problem with STERBs is that they are *short-term*. They do not last, and they do not deal with the true emotional issue. And lastly, they do nothing to remove the cork that is jammed in the spout. In fact, most people don't even realize that there *is* a cork in the spout.

Eventually, our steam kettle is overloaded and the STERBs no longer create the illusion of well-being. Imagine what might happen if a major loss event, a death or divorce, were added to this collection of unresolved emotions. It might put such a strain on our corked kettle as to cause an explosion.

While some emotional explosions are huge and make national headlines, most are much smaller. Here is an unfair question. Have you ever had an emotional explosion larger than circumstances called for? Sadly, we know that you all have to say yes. Over time, we develop the habit of putting a cork in our own personal steam kettles. We bottle up our feelings because we have been taught to do so.

The actions of grief recovery will help you remove the cork. You will then be able to deal more effectively with the emotions associated with loss. In order to remove the cork, we will look at all of the ideas that created it and replace them with more accurate ideas about dealing with sad, painful, and negative emotions.

A simple analogy: if your yard is full of weeds, you can cut the weeds to give some short-term relief, but they will grow back. Or you can pull the weeds and eliminate the problem. You are arriving at the point of making a decision: short-term or long-term relief. We want you to commit to long-term relief. And we will guide you and help you along the way.

IDENTIFYING YOUR SHORT-TERM ENERGY-RELIEVING BEHAVIORS

Russell had never been much of a drinker. Even though he had been in the restaurant business most of his adult life, he rarely drank and never got drunk. Following his second divorce, he found himself going to a friend's bar and having one or two drinks every night. This behavior was reinforced by the friendliness at the bar. After about three months, this nightly ritual didn't seem to help anymore. He stopped drinking and started going home every night and reading escapist mystery novels. He substituted one short-term action for another. This was a classic example of short-term energy-relieving behavior.

SECOND HOMEWORK ASSIGNMENT

The homework assignment (for both partners and those working alone) is to identify the short-term energy-relieving actions you have used or may be using to escape the pain caused by your losses.

After reading the chapter again, try to identify at least two examples of short-term relief you have used to displace your feelings. This is not as easy as it appears. It could be your first chance to demonstrate your commitment to total honesty.

Here is the list of short-term energy-relieving behaviors from earlier in the chapter. Use it as a guideline to help determine whether you have been relying on short-term relief.

- Food
- Alcohol/Drugs
- Anger
- Exercise
- Fantasy (movies, TV, books)
- Isolation
- Sex
- Shopping (humorously called Retail Therapy)
- Workaholism

Using a clean sheet of paper, write down the short-term energy relievers in which you have participated. Then add any others that you discover. It is actually very common in our society to have been socialized with the idea that we should cover up emotional pain rather than confront it directly.

THIRD PARTNERS MEETING

Begin by reaffirming your commitments to total honesty, absolute confidentiality, and the uniqueness of your individual recovery. As always, meet in a private place where you will not feel uncomfortable if you cry. Have tissues handy.

Short-term energy-relieving behaviors (STERBs) can be a fun category for partners to talk about. However, it can also be painful and awkward. Be especially careful not to judge, criticize, or evaluate your partner (or yourself). Be mindful of your commitment to absolute confidentiality. Maintaining truth and safety is essential to recovery.

Read your list of STERBs. It is important to remember why we participate in them. It is not because we are defective, but because we were taught to do so.

One of the purposes of this exercise is to help you become aware of things that you may have been doing unconsciously. The possibility of changing some of the habits that hurt you lies in becoming aware that they exist.

After you have each had a turn, set the time and place for your next meeting.

For Those Working Alone

Read the chapter again. Examine both the general and the specific ways in which you have used STERBs in your life to cope with loss.

Another awkward question: "Is it possible that one of my major short-term energy relievers is *isolation*? Is that another reason I'm working without a partner?"

It may seem like we are pressuring you. In fact, we are

sharing many years of experience. Most people who have difficulty finding a partner are merely afraid that a potential partner would refuse them. We cannot tell you that this would not happen, but please reconsider your choice of working alone. We will not mention this again.

9

The Loss History Graph

Now that you've established that myths, intellect, and short-term energy-relieving behaviors have not been providing the kind of long-term benefits needed, you might have begun to feel stuck. This is the point at which you may have started to "act recovered." That's when you say, "I'm fine," when you really mean, "I'm hurting." This is a dangerous place to wind up.

If there were some magical way that we could lift the pain of your losses off your shoulders, we would. But we can't, so we'll do the next best thing. We will teach you how to complete your relationship to the pain caused by the loss.

The loss history graph is designed to help you discover what losses have occurred in your life and which of them are most restricting your day-to-day living. At first glance, it might seem strange for us to tell you that you need to identify the losses in your life. After all, shouldn't you know what they are? Sadly, many people, particularly when they were young, were taught to compare losses and minimize feelings. Thus, they may not be aware of the emotions they have from past events that continue to limit their lives.

COMPARE AND MINIMIZE

Somewhere during your formative years, you heard the statement, "I cried because I had no shoes until I met a man who had no feet." Clearly, this statement is designed to get people to pause and be grateful for what they have rather than focus on what they don't have. While that is an admirable quality, it is often construed to mean, "Compare losses to minimize feelings."

Russell remembers a dinner party where he was seated next to two women friends. One woman's husband had died of cancer several months earlier. The other woman was in the middle of a painful divorce. Russell asked her how she was doing. She whispered, "Terrible, but I can't feel bad about my divorce because her husband died." This is a perfect example of compare and minimize.

LOSS HISTORY GRAPH EXAMPLES

Once we establish a habit, we continue to use it unconsciously. Our lives are made up of many habits. You've probably been putting on the same shoe first all your life and never thought about it until right now. This is also probably true of how you've been trying to deal with the losses in your life. That's why a Loss History Graph is so important. We need to know what our pattern is so we can confront and change it.

The primary purpose of this exercise is to create a detailed examination of the loss events in your life and to identify the patterns that have resulted from them. There are several other reasons for making a Loss History Graph. One is to bring everything up to the surface where we can look at it. Buried or forgotten losses can extend the pain and frustration associated with unresolved grief. Another is to practice being totally truthful. We can often be dishonest without ever lying. That is, we omit things and thereby create an inaccurate picture. An additional benefit of using this exercise is observing which short-term relievers we have relied upon after losses.

We're all going to have other losses during our lives, and we don't want to fall into the same old traps. As the old mountain man told the young mountain man, "If you want to avoid bear traps, it's a good idea to know what they look like."

In order to do a Loss History Graph, it's a good idea to know what it looks like. Here are ours.

JOHN W. JAMES
BORN: *February 16, 1944*

'49 Puppies—As a starting point, I'll tell you about my dawn of conscious memory. My first memory is from the day our family dog gave birth to a litter of puppies. Late one night, after my brother and I had gone to sleep, our father woke us up. He took us to the dog's bed. Our dog, who had always been friendly, seemed to be suspicious and wary. I remember being a little frightened. As my dad brought us closer to the bed, I could see three or four little lumps near her. Soon she began to whine and move around. I thought that she was in pain and wanted to help her. My father told us to stay back, that she was having trouble delivering one of the puppies. When he said that, it dawned on me what the little lumps were. I was happy, scared, proud, and confused all at the same time. Eventually, my father had to help her give birth to the last three puppies.

My brother and I wanted to hold and pet the puppies right away, but we were told that our dog might not like that, so we went back to bed. Of course, we couldn't sleep and spent half the night talking about this wondrous event. The next two weeks were spent being solicitous of our dog and waiting for the puppies to open their eyes.

This event is the very first conscious memory that I've been able to identify. I have no earlier recollection of anything.

'50 Dog—My dog died (as discussed in chapter 3).

'53 Moving—This was the year we moved for the first time. Moving is a major loss for children. My parents explained all the intellectual reasons why we were moving: we would live in a better neighborhood and a better house, it was closer to school, and we would own it rather than rent. That didn't make the move feel any better. I was going to miss my friends.

'58 Grandfather—My grandfather died.

'62 Girlfriend—My girlfriend and I broke up.

'64/65 Vietnam—The way Vietnam veterans were treated in our society reinforced the loss-of-trust experience. It is this loss of trust that causes so many problems for veterans even to this day. As a society, we have paid and are still paying dearly for this. During the years of the war, we suffered the deaths of more than fifty-eight thousand combat troops; in the years since the war ended, we have felt the loss by suicide of more than three times that number.

'66 Father—My father died. I had seen him only once since I came home from overseas; much was unfinished in our relationship. His drinking had continued until it finally killed him. It was a very painful experience for me.

'69 Brother—My younger brother, a twenty-year-old pole vaulter at Southern Illinois University, was in perfect health when he died. He was on his way to visit me in southern California, where I lived at the time. He was traveling with two of his friends from college; they'd stopped for the night and had all decided to take a nap. Later that afternoon, when his friends went to wake him, they found that he had died.

I spent days trying to find some intellectual reason for his death, and when I couldn't find one, I assigned blame for his death to God.

'77 Son—My son died. Two years earlier, my wife and I had had a daughter. Her arrival was the high point of my life. When my wife became pregnant again, I was looking forward to another such experience. About five months into the pregnancy, complications set in. When my wife went into premature labor, we raced to the hospital, where every possible medical technique was employed to slow or stop the process. She was hooked up to monitoring devices, and for two days we had to listen to a perfectly healthy heartbeat while knowing there was little chance the child would live.

All of my life I had been taught to believe certain things about what my job was as a man, a husband, and a father. I had been taught to believe that it was my job to identify problems and solve them. What I discovered right away was that it did not matter who I knew, what I knew, how much money I had, or how intelligent I was—there was nothing I could do. It was the most frustrating experience I had ever had.

Despite all the medical intervention, our son was born. For the first eight hours, it appeared that everything would be all right. Then things started to go wrong. Once again, identifying the problem was easy. I could see the problem: he weighed about two pounds, had black hair, and was encased in a glass box. But there was nothing I could do but stand and look at all the monitoring equipment and feel impotent.

This went on for two days. I was trying to help my wife because that was what I had been taught to do. There is nothing wrong with that except, in trying to help her, I was not acknowledging my own pain. At the end of the second day, my son just breathed out and never breathed in again.

If you can believe this, it started to go downhill from there. The things people said and did were shocking. That my wife and I were unable to talk became apparent. Our relationship began to fall apart immediately. During the next eight months, I went everywhere, talked to everyone, and read everything that I could get my hands on to help ease the pain. This was the point where I discovered there was little or no help available to deal with the grief. That was real despair.

'78 Divorce—My wife and I were divorced. The divorce happened because we had no idea how to deal with the grief caused by all the changes in our lives. We were newly married, new parents, and new grievers, all at the same time. The death of our son was the straw that broke the camel's back.

In typical griever fashion, my mind was preoccupied with thoughts of what I wished I had done *different, better, or more*. If I hadn't made the cost of medical bills such an issue, my wife might have gone for checkups more frequently. The night the emergency started, we had no baby-sitter and no real idea of the seriousness of my wife's condition, so I didn't go with her to the doctor's office. I used to sit and think about how frightening that must have been for her. Even as all of these thoughts were running through my mind, I had no skill or practice at being able to talk about what I was feeling. I felt isolated and alone, yet I truly believed that I was supposed to be strong and keep it all inside. Since that was all I knew, that is what I did. With that type of pressure building up, arguments became common. Hurt feelings were then added to the fire, and more arguments followed. At the same time, my wife was thinking that if she hadn't gotten pregnant so soon after the birth of our daughter, then none of this would have happened. That was her *different, better, or more* thinking. She too had no knowledge about the importance of talking about her feelings.

When communication breaks down in a marriage, no matter the cause, it is only a matter of time before divorce occurs. When the divorce takes place, we have yet another grieving experience to deal with, so the cycle continues.

While writing this book, I called my former wife to discuss her thoughts about telling this part of the story. One of the things she shared with me was the fact that she had not known for several years how much the death of our son affected me. How could she have possibly known? I was an academy award griever then.

Setting out to do a Loss History Graph can be a scary proposition. So before we ask you to do this exercise, we want you to see another example.

Here is Russell's loss history graph.

RUSSELL FRIEDMAN
BORN: *January 4, 1943*

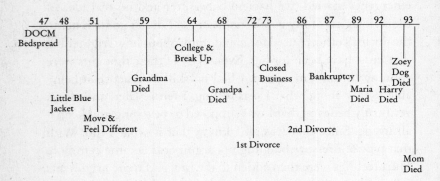

'47 *Dawn of Conscious Memory*—My first conscious memory is neither happy nor sad. It is a simple memory of a blue bedspread. It was covered with nautical designs.

'48 *Little Blue Jacket*—My father took me to a Rochester Royals basketball game. At the game, he bought me a Royals jacket. Some time later, I lost the jacket. When my father found out that the jacket was lost, he berated me for losing it. I remember feeling as if my father was no longer safe for me. After several other incidents of this type, I did not trust him anymore.

'51 *Feeling Different, Plus Major Move*—I was born allergic to milk, eggs, nuts, and chocolate. One of the consequences of the allergies was the need to have special food when I went to school. I felt very different from the other kids in my class. I also had very, very red hair, and approximately two and a half million freckles. That may sound cute. But as the possessor, it did not feel cute. I was teased often and sometimes cruelly by the other children. I did not have the wherewithal to defend myself. I just felt so terribly different.

We lived in Rochester, New York, which gets very cold and damp in the winters. I suffered with asthma. It was so serious that my parents were advised to move to either Arizona or Florida for the heat. I did not want to leave my friends and the neighborhood to which I had grown accustomed. I made an emotional appeal to my parents. My appeal was met with intellectual explanations about a better school, a bigger house, and Daddy having a better job. My presenting emotions about my friends were never addressed.

We moved to Florida. In Florida, another physical problem surfaced that has had lifelong consequences. Having red hair and very light skin, Miami's intense heat and deadly ultraviolet rays had an immediate impact on my life. I was forced to wear shirts in the swimming pool and zinc oxide on my face so I could play outdoors. I suffered a few serious sunburns and also developed a fear of the sun. It started to affect my choice of activities, affecting in turn my friendships with my peers. The bottom line for me was that my red hair, fair skin, and freckles made me feel very *different* from everyone else.

'57 Grandma—Grandma died. She had been living with us since my mom had gone back to work. Grandma was the primary caretaker for my brother, who is ten years younger than me. This is where I learned to "be strong for others."

'64 Broken Engagement—This was my first full-fledged love affair, with major plans for marriage and children. When it crashed and burned, I was devastated. I had absolutely no ideas, tools, or skills to help me deal with the intense emotional pain. I was in my last year of college. I cut classes. I stared at walls. I just went through the motions.

'64 College Graduation—Traditionally, graduations are perceived as positive experiences. And that is at least half true. I
was torn, however, between the excitement and freedom of
my new adult status and the sadness of leaving behind four
years of people and places and familiarity. No one wanted to
hear about or acknowledge the sad part.

'68 Grandpa—Grandpa died. I was not fond of my grandfather. He was very gruff, and I was scared of him. Even as I
got older, I found his manner threatening. When he died, he
and his son, my dad, had not been on good terms. I tried to
"be strong" for my dad.

'72 First Divorce—This divorce was totally unexpected for
me. I did not have an inkling that it might happen. I was devastated. I was confused. I was totally lost. The only tool I had
for dealing with any kind of loss was "be strong for others."
But this was me. *I was the other*. As I look back on it, I am
amazed that I am alive. I cannot imagine how I drove a
car without accidentally killing myself or anybody else. It was
almost impossible for me to concentrate. Even then, I knew
that this loss was not singular. I had a sense that in addition to
the loss of the marriage, there was the loss of all my hopes,
dreams, and expectations, coupled with a massive "loss of
trust." Since trust had always been a major problem for me,
this divorce and how it happened crushed what little trust I
had left.

'73 Closed Business—When my wife and I divorced, I kept
the restaurant we had opened together. I was preoccupied
with the emotions caused by the divorce. I had no effective
skills for dealing with those painful emotions. While I had
normally been a fairly attentive entrepreneur, my concentration was greatly diminished. I started making some very poor
business decisions, which, in turn, led to poorer ones. In the

end, I closed the business down. My heart was not in it anymore.

'86 Second Divorce—This divorce was very different from the first one. The pain was intense. In addition to the death of the relationship and the hopes and dreams, another factor troubled me greatly. I was forty-three years old. My sense of myself, my life, and my future was different from what it had been after my first divorce. I was older. My business was in a neighborhood populated with elderly people. I used to sit and stare at the elderly couples, thinking, "When do I get to go off into the sunset with someone?" My parents and my wife's parents were still together. I was 0 for 2 in marriage. I felt like a complete failure.

'87 Bankruptcy—Having experienced a first divorce and closing a business in response to it did not prepare me for the second divorce and the financial tragedy that followed. In fact, the earlier events almost predicted the later ones. I was practiced at divorce, so I got another one. I was practiced at business failure, so I failed again. In neither case had I experienced recovery or completion of the emotions caused by the losses. The cumulative unresolved feelings created a massive preoccupation from which I made one horrible business decision after another. I had no alternative but to declare bankruptcy. Having been socialized to be the provider, the bankruptcy caused me to feel like the biggest "loser" on the planet.

'89 Marie—Marie, my girlfriend's mother, died. We had become quite close. I loved the way she asked me how I was doing and then really listened to my answer. By the time Marie died, I had begun working at the Grief Recovery Institute. More important, I had completed my relationship to the pain caused by the prior loss experiences in my life. My personal completions allowed two different things to occur.

First, I was as complete as I knew how to be with Marie while she was still alive. Second, I was really affected by her death. Having completed earlier relationships, my heart was open to new ones. Being open means that painful things hurt. That same openness had allowed me to be more loving. Sadness being the normal and healthy reaction to loss, Marie's death hurt my heart.

'92 Harry—Harry, my girlfriend's father, died. He and I had become very close after his wife, Marie, died. We spent countless hours on the couch at his house or my house watching every possible sporting event. He was eighty-seven, but he had an amazingly critical eye for all the details of each sport. He also had a wealth of knowledge of sporting events from before I was born. It was often like a fun history lesson for me. As fate would have it, Harry died just a few days before the Super Bowl. There was a very empty seat on my couch on Super Bowl Sunday.

'93 Dog Zoey—Our dog Zoey died. She was a 100-pound lap dog. (If a 100-pound dog wants to sit on your lap, you don't argue with her.) She was zany and wonderful, and as with many relationships with pets, mine with her was unconditionally loving. She had been with my girlfriend and her daughter since she was a puppy. When I moved in, she adopted me and trained me. When she got cancer, we tried everything, but to no avail. As I arrived home each evening shortly after she had died, my heart would fall to my feet as soon as the garage door started up. Those moments when I remembered that Zoey would not be at the top of the stairs to greet me were among the most painful I have experienced.

'93 Mom—The day before Thanksgiving, suddenly and unexpectedly, my mother died. Let me try to describe for you

what I experienced in the moments after I was told that she had died. I had walked into my office around 11:00 A.M., having just finished an early morning round of golf. As I walked through the office doorway, my assistant stood up and said, "Russell, I have terrible news, your mother has died!" I felt as if I had been hit in the chest with enough force to knock me down—my knees buckled and I started crying. As my legs sagged, my assistant and another friend surrounded me and held me up. I fell into their arms and sobbed and sobbed.

WHAT GOES ON THE LOSS HISTORY GRAPH

Since most of us relate the words *grief* and *loss* primarily to death and perhaps to divorce, let's establish which human experiences come under the heading of grief. Here is the most helpful definition we use: *Grief is the conflicting group of human emotions caused by an end to or change in a familiar pattern of behavior*. Thus, any changes in relationships to people, place, or events can cause the conflicting feelings we call grief.

Look at how many other loss events are also covered by this definition. Think about moving. When we move, every single familiar pattern may change. Where we live, where we work, and who we regularly see all change. Major financial changes, positive or negative, create massive changes in our familiar patterns. Major changes in bodily functions or abilities can have enormous grief consequences. Losing the use of limbs or eyesight or a condition like diabetes or kidney failure automatically alters familiar patterns. Strokes and heart attacks often affect how and when we exercise and what and when we eat. Menopause can cause huge feelings of loss for women as well as for their mates. Divorce is somewhat obvious when it is our own. We are also affected by the divorce of anyone we are close to—parent, child, sibling, or other.

Childhood issues of mistreatment—physical, sexual, or emotional—often set up patterns wherein positive interactions are sabotaged because they are not as "familiar" as negative interactions.

Many life experiences fit our definition of grief. Almost anything that has affected you negatively is a grieving experience for you. When you read John's and Russell's Loss History Graphs, you got some idea of which life events are losses. Generally speaking, if you think something was a loss, put it on your graph. You can't really make a mistake in this exercise.

THIRD HOMEWORK ASSIGNMENT: PREPARING YOUR LOSS HISTORY GRAPH

With all of the preambles out of the way, it is time to begin. We will give you (both partners and those working alone) the instructions for the Loss History Graph exercise just as we do in our seminars.

1: The entire exercise should not take you more than an hour. You may experience a wide range of emotional responses as the result of doing the Loss History Graph. Or you may have little or no emotional response. That is perfectly okay, do not be alarmed. Have a box of tissues handy. If you have an emotional reaction, let it be okay with you.

2: The writing part of the exercise is nonverbal. It is best done alone and in silence.

3: Get a pen or pencil and a piece of blank paper, at least the size of typing paper or standard notebook paper (8½" x 11"); legal-size paper (8½" x 14") is even better. Place the paper horizontally on your desk or table.

4: Draw a straight line across the center of the page. Then divide your line into four equal parts, marking the sections lightly with a pencil. This will give you reference points for plotting dates.

Birthdate   Mid Point   Current Year

└─────────•────────────•────────────•─────────┘

5: For example, if you are fifty years old, at the halfway point you were twenty-five. Write the year of your birth at the left end of the line. Write the current date on the right end of the line. Then plot your dawn of conscious memory, or earliest recollection, whether you perceive it as a loss or not, and mark it just after the year you were born.

6: Our examples began with our earliest conscious memory. If you think hard, you'll find that your first recollection will most likely fall between ages two and five, probably closer to five. It may be good or bad, happy or sad; it may be an event, an experience, an object, or a place. One of the easiest ways to establish an effective dawn-of-conscious-memory date is to remember something about your first house. Do not spend an inordinate amount of time establishing your dawn-of-conscious-memory date. It is merely a starting point.

7: You do not need to get the dates exactly right. We are much more interested in your emotional response to your losses.

8: Now take a few moments and ask yourself, "What is the most painful, life-limiting loss I have ever experienced?"

TIME AND INTENSITY

All losses are experienced at 100 percent intensity when they occur. As we reflect, we recognize that some losses have had a greater impact on us than others. We have referred to the fact that relationships are composed of both time and intensity. Here is what we mean.

Russell had gone to the same dry cleaner, twice a week, for ten years. The same lady took his shirts and his money each time. He didn't know her name, so he referred to her as "the lady." One day when Russell went to pick up his shirts, a man came and took care of him. Russell said, "Where's the lady?" "Oh, she died." Russell felt a sense of sadness even though he had not known her name, nor anything about her. That relationship, although of many years' duration, had almost no intensity.

Russell was engaged to a young woman in 1964. This passionate relationship lasted only three months. When the romance crashed and burned, the two of them were not on good terms. He never spoke to her again. Thirty-two years later, Russell got a call from a mutual friend saying that she had died. This news had a powerful impact on him. The relationship, while short, had had tremendous emotional intensity.

1: Identify your most painful loss. Find the approximate date point on your horizontal line and draw a vertical line downward to the bottom of the page. Make a notation of what the loss was: "Mom died," "Child died," "Divorce." You don't have to spend too much time writing out at length each separate grieving experience, as we did in our examples. Just make simple notes of words or phrases that will remind you of the loss.

2: After establishing and plotting your most painful loss experience, let your mind go back to your earliest memories and start marking down the loss events you remember. Use the length of the vertical line to establish the relative degree of intensity of the loss. Always make short notes so you will be able to recall what the loss was; for example, "Dog died," or, "Lost business."

Occasionally, you may realize that you have had both positive and negative responses to the same experiences. This is totally normal. For many people, their wedding day is simultaneously the most exciting of all days while also representing a "loss of freedom." The birth of a child can be exhilarating, on the one hand, and terrifying, on the other, as the parents take on new responsibilities. For the purposes of this exercise, however, we are focusing on the sad, negative, or painful aspects of these events. Grievers will often try to deal only with the positive side, so as to avoid the painful. That's one of the reasons you are using this book, so even if it seems uncomfortable, please stay with the loss perspective only.

If you find that a half-hour has gone by and all you have plotted is your dawn of conscious memory and one other loss, then take a break. Sometimes we try a little too hard and get stuck. Look back at John's and Russell's graphs. Their graphs will remind you of some of your losses.

It is not at all unnatural to sense some resistance in yourself. Remember, persistence will pay off in the long run. Our experience has shown us that most people over the age of fourteen have at least five losses to plot. For adults, the average is between ten and fifteen loss experiences.

Don't try to get this "right." Just be honest. There are no grades given for this work, and no one's approval is required. Abandon yourself to the exercise, and you will receive benefit directly proportional to the amount you put into it. But first, and now, you must begin!

LEARNING FROM YOUR LOSS HISTORY GRAPH

Congratulations on finishing your graph!

The story of your life can be an eye-opening experience. It is imperative that you look at your losses to discover what misinformation you were taught directly or absorbed indirectly. It is equally essential that you not judge, evaluate, or criticize yourself for what you were shown or for interpretations you made.

Your first commitment in this regard is to be gentle with yourself about the discoveries you make. It can also be helpful to suspend judgment and criticism of those who taught you any incorrect ideas. Don't worry, you will have ample opportunity later to complete any thoughts and feelings about the sources of misinformation.

Having finished the graph, it is now time to examine it and see what you can learn. From your dawn of conscious memory onward, you may be able to get some very clear pictures about what you were influenced to believe. For those of you working with partners, you will soon see how many parallels there usually are between grieving people. In our seminars and outreach programs, people are often amazed at the losses and attitudes they have in common. While there are many parallels, we are still individuals. Scientists tell us that no two snowflakes, crystals, or grains of sand are alike, but they are made of the same ingredients. People are also unique. This exercise helps illustrate our human similarities and differences.

For those of you working alone, you might notice that some of your losses and attitudes are similar to some of John's and Russell's.

FOURTH PARTNERS MEETING

Begin by reaffirming your commitments to total honesty, absolute confidentiality, and the uniqueness of your individual recovery. As always, meet in a private place where you will not feel uncomfortable if you cry. Have tissues handy.

This meeting marks a change in how you will proceed. These new guidelines will carry you through the balance of your meetings. Read them very carefully. Successful completion hinges on following these instructions.

Working with a partner does have benefits. One is the ability to verbalize what you have written. In order for this exercise to have the maximum value, we will give you some very strong guidelines, which we have developed over twenty years. We suggest that you adhere to them.

Make sure you bring your Loss History Graph and the two lists—on misinformation and short-term energy-relieving behaviors—that you've already discussed.

Instructions for the Listening Partner
1. Sit a reasonable distance away. Avoid a sense of being in your partner's face or smothering him or her.
2. As the listening partner, you may laugh or cry, if appropriate, but *you may not talk!*
3. Do not touch your partner. Touch usually stops feelings.
4. Remember the image of being a heart with ears. Do your best to stay in the moment and really listen to your partner's story.

Instructions for the Talking Partner
1. Try to tell your loss history graph in half an hour or less. This is not a rigid rule, but be careful not to turn the entire meeting into a long monologue, which would have no value for you.
2. If you cry, try to keep talking while you cry. Push the words up and out, rather than swallowing them. People tend to choke off feelings in their throat.
3. When you finish your graph, ask your partner for a hug (assuming you've made hugs safe).
4. After getting your hug, take a few minutes to talk again about the misinformation you learned following your losses

as well as the short-term energy-relieving behaviors you may have participated in. This is an ideal opportunity to see the connection between your beliefs and the limits they may have put on your recovery.

Take a little break, and then let your partner do his or her graph.

Make plans for your next meeting.

For Those Working Alone

Since you are working alone, you may find it effective to use John's and Russell's Loss History Graphs as your silent partner. Reread theirs, then look at yours. Notice the similarities and the differences. Once again, look at your STERBs. See if you notice any connection between your short-term relievers and your losses. Look at your lists of myths and beliefs to see whether they connect to the losses you have graphed.

PART THREE

Finding the Solution

Welcome to the third and final part of this handbook. The solution is made up of five actions you must take in order to complete the pain caused by significant emotional loss. The actions that follow will require open-mindedness, much willingness, and courage. These actions and their meanings are:

1. Gaining awareness—that an incomplete emotional relationship exists.
2. Accepting responsibility—that in part you are the cause of the incompleteness.
3. Identifying recovery communications—that you have not delivered.
4. Taking actions—to communicate them.
5. Moving beyond loss—saying good-bye to undelivered communications and to pain.

10

What Is Incompleteness?

Throughout this book we have referred to how we do things in our seminars. Most of the exercises translate easily into a format appropriate to a book, but some things require a little more explanation. One of them is coming to an understanding of exactly what constitutes emotional incompleteness.

In our three-day seminar for grievers, we are able to illustrate incompleteness by asking a few questions. On the second day, we ask one person whether he or she has had any positive thoughts or feelings about one of the other participants. When the answer is yes, we ask what the positive idea was. Usually it is something like, "I admired her courage," or, "I liked his openness." We ask, "Did you tell him?" The respondent says no. Then we ask, "What if he had died before you told him? Who would be left with the undelivered communication?" The response: "I would." Then we ask, "If you became incomplete with a stranger in one day, what have you done over a lifetime with family members, friends, and others?"

Incompleteness is not limited to major events. It is an accumulation of undelivered communications, large and small, that have emotional value to you. To the best of our knowledge, only the living grieve. It is essential that we complete what is unfinished for us.

Sometimes incompleteness is caused by our actions or nonactions. Other times it is caused by circumstances outside of our control.

One sad story illustrates unfinished emotions caused by circumstances.

A young boy ran across the front yard, hurrying to catch the school bus. As he ran, his mom yelled from the front porch, "Timmy, tuck in your shirt, what will the neighbors think?" Several hours later, the police knocked on the mother's front door. Her son Timmy had been killed in a freak accident in the schoolyard.

In addition to the unimaginable pain that the mother was suffering, which last communication do you think she wished had been different? We are not suggesting that if her last interaction with Timmy had been different, she would have felt any less pain. What we are suggesting is her last remark to her son definitely fits into the category of things we wish had ended *different, better, or more. We rarely ever know which interaction will be our last.* It is not abnormal in many of our relationships to table a few topics that we plan to deal with later. This is not necessarily procrastination, just a plan for later. But following a death or a divorce, such postponements often are some of the ingredients of incompleteness.

While death and divorce are obvious arenas for incomplete emotions, what about other losses? Often when we look back on difficult relationships with living people—parents, siblings, and others—we recognize many things that we wish had been *different, better, or more*. All too frequently, it is the accumulation of undelivered communications that limits us in these relationships as well.

Sometimes incompleteness is caused or exaggerated by others. Some people will not allow us to say meaningful things to them. Since we cannot force them to listen to us, we often get trapped with these undelivered communications, both positive and negative. Sometimes we are afraid to say emotionally charged things. Or we have been waiting for the right moment or circumstances. Sometimes the right time never comes. Or we forget. Or we get sidetracked. And then someone dies. And we are stuck with the undelivered emotional communication.

In short, emotional incompleteness is any undelivered emotional communication. Sometimes we're not sure what we said or did. This can cause feelings of incompleteness. Sometimes we are not sure whether the other person heard us, or whether they received our communication the way we intended. This also can leave us feeling unfinished.

Please hear this. Being emotionally incomplete does not mean that you are bad. It does not mean that you are defective. It only means that a variety of circumstances and actions or nonactions have robbed you of the opportunity to be complete.

HOW TO IDENTIFY WHAT IS INCOMPLETE

In essence, your Loss History Graph was an itemization of past grieving experiences. At the end of this section are instructions for using your Loss History Graph to help identify which loss or losses are still emotionally incomplete. As you look at your Loss History Graph, you may sense a wide range of emotions attached to the people, the events, and the relationships listed there. When reminded of a loss, you might feel sad. This is entirely normal.

Your objective is to discover those relationships that are incomplete. In order to do so, it is helpful if you can try to distinguish between pain and sadness. Some of the clues that might help you are:

1. If you are unwilling to think about or talk about someone who has died, or any other loss, that may signify unresolved grief.
2. If fond memories turn painful, you may be experiencing unresolved grief.
3. If you want to talk only about positive aspects of the relationship, it might be unresolved grief.
4. Wanting to talk only about negative aspects of the relationship may be a sign of unresolved grief.
5. Unresolved grief may be at the root of any fear associated with thoughts or feelings about the relationship.

We have feelings in response to every life change that occurs. Most of these changes are small and insignificant and cause little or no discomfort. Yet some have had a lasting impact on our attitudes and outlooks on life. The more intense these feelings are, the higher the probability that they are unresolved or incomplete.

Motivation to attend our seminars and outreach programs is usually prompted by a recent loss. The actions of recovery usually lead to an awareness that you have other incomplete relationships. You may make a similar discovery as you work through this book.

CHOOSING A LOSS TO COMPLETE

You are ready to identify the loss that is most incomplete for you. While it could be a death, remember, loss is not limited to death. For most people, divorce implies emotional incompleteness. Many of our relationships with living people—parents, siblings, other relatives, friends—may also be incomplete.

Instructions

1. Get out your Loss History Graph. Circle the losses with which you think you might still be incomplete. Be honest in your assessment. It doesn't matter how many losses you list or how long ago they happened. If you don't know whether you're incomplete with respect to a loss on your graph, circle it.

2. Use the idea of time and/or intensity coupled with your own honest sense of what is unfinished or what is still painful for you. Be realistic here. If your infant died, the relationship may not have had much time but will certainly have had tremendous intensity. Therefore, the death of your child might be the correct first choice for you.

3. There is a strong possibility that the loss that brought you to this book may not be the one you wind up working on first. If that occurs, let it be okay. However, we don't want you to choose a less intense loss out of fear or avoidance of a more painful one.

4. The loss that is most incomplete for you may not appear on your Loss History Graph. Be alert to the fact that your most incomplete relationship might be with a living person who does not appear as a "loss."

5. Don't spend more than an hour in this process of elimination. You will confuse yourself. The real question is simply,

"Which of the losses in my life is limiting and restricting me the most right now?"

6. Choose one. You cannot make a major error in choosing which relationship to work on. If there are several incomplete relationships in your life, you will eventually work on them all. *Note: You cannot do your parents together. You must do each relationship, one at a time.* For now, we want you to choose the relationship that seems to embody the most pain or the most unfinished emotion, or both.

11

Introducing the Relationship Graph

To create an accurate memory picture of a relationship, it is helpful to use a clear-cut format. Over the years we have developed an extremely simple process that is very likely to help you discover what is unfinished for you.

As always, we recommend that you not take shortcuts. If you use the format exactly as suggested, it is almost always successful. In fact, most problems occur when someone tries to change the format.

THE RELATIONSHIP GRAPH IS DIFFERENT FROM THE LOSS HISTORY GRAPH

In the Loss History Graph, we focused on loss; we listed sad, painful, or negative life events that we remembered. The point of the Relationship Graph is to take a complete and detailed look at one relationship. Positive or happy events are marked above the center line, and negative or sad events below the line.

At some point after a loss occurs, our brains begin a review, searching for what was never communicated or completed. You may or may not be aware that this review began very soon after the loss. In fact, the review continues intermittently until the loss is completed. The purpose of the Relationship Graph is to help you tap into that review and use it to discover what is unfinished for you so that you can then complete it.

COMPLETING IS NOT FORGETTING

To resolve an emotionally incomplete loss, you must complete it. Completing does not mean that you will forget your loved one. What we are completing is our relationship to the pain caused by the loss. We are completing anything that was left unfinished at the time of the loss. The only thing that can stop you now is the fear that you'll forget your loved one. *That is not possible.*

The three aspects of relationships that we focus on are physical, emotional, and spiritual.

Death ends the physical relationship we had. We can no longer touch or speak to the other person in the same way. Divorce dramatically changes the physical relationship we had with our spouse. We do not touch them or even talk with them in the same way.

Emotional relationships include all of the feelings we may have about another person or even a pet. Those feelings are not limited to happy or positive but include painful and negative emotions. When a death or divorce occurs, we must discover and complete whatever is incomplete at the time of the loss. While the physical relationship ended or changed, the emotional relationship continues in our memory.

The spiritual aspect of our relationships is more difficult to define. We all have differing ideas about spirituality. For our purposes, spiritual aspects are those that are neither physical nor emotional. It is that intangible something that makes you sense a connection to others. Your spiritual connection also does not end when a death or divorce occurs.

Since grief is the normal and natural emotional response to loss, the vast majority of this book relates to emotions. Successful completion of unfinished emotions allows us to become complete with the often painful reality that the physical relationship has ended.

Grief recovery affects the quality of your life. Completion of unfinished emotions does not interfere with any religious, philosophical, or spiritual beliefs you may have about seeing someone again in heaven.

ACCURATE MEMORY PICTURES: YOUR PART

We talked about grievers having a tendency to create larger-than-life memory pictures. It is unlikely that you would be able to complete with someone you consider a saint or a devil. You can complete your loss only by acknowledging the truth. If you recall, the first commitment you made in this book was to tell the truth. Enshrinement or bedevilment is *not the truth*.

We've talked to grievers following the death of a loved one, and in no time at all they began telling us about someone who never made a mistake in his or her entire life. They talk only about the good and positive aspects of their loved one. When we listen closely, we'll even hear: "I should have appreciated him more while I had him. He was a perfect husband." We have heard the same kind of comments following the breakup of long-term romantic relationships and marriages. *This kind of exaggerated, one-sided memory is really the function of a broken heart that does not know a better way to communicate the truth.*

As much as you love the person who died, or even the person you are divorced from, he or she was not perfect—as you are not perfect. Every relationship, even the most ideal, has its ups and downs. When you are taking these grief recovery actions, you can only be responsible for your part. If you're remembering your loved ones as you wish they were, not as they truly were, it becomes impossible to complete your emotional relationship with them. An accurate memory of your loved ones is much stronger and will be cherished more than a fantasy about them.

TRUTH IS THE KEY TO RECOVERY

The essence of recovery is contained in the premise of being totally honest about *ourselves* in relation to others. However, as humans, it is virtually impossible not to have impressions and opinions about others. So we must allow that our perception of others may limit or restrict our recovery. Being supercritical of what others did or did not do usually leads to an inaccurate appraisal of our relationship with them.

It may seem that this book is overly directed at helping people complete their relationship with a "loved one" who has died. We're sure there are many people reading this book who still grieve about someone they didn't like. Your feelings may be ones of strong resentment or even hate. Even so, this program of grief recovery will work for you. We will have more to say about resentments in relationships as we progress through the recovery actions.

We are going to take an in-depth look at a relationship with an eye to discovering what we wish had ended *different, better, or more*, as well as the unrealized hopes, dreams, and expectations about the future. We will be looking for the things we wish we had said or not said. We will be looking for the things we wish we had done or not done. And we will be looking for the things we wish the other person had said or done.

Some relationships are more loving than others. Indeed, some relationships are more complete than others. However, we have yet to meet anyone who had no undelivered emotional communications at all. We have met people who were afraid or unwilling to look honestly at their own part of what might have been unfinished. We have met people who had so much misinformation as to believe that anything honest they might say could hurt someone who had died.

Let us reemphasize at this point that the motive is not to hurt or destroy memories or relationships. This remains a private acknowledgment, confined to yourself or to a partner who is sworn to confidentiality.

EVEN LONG ILLNESSES END IN UNFINISHED BUSINESS

Question: After a long-term illness, during which you took care of your dying loved one twenty-four hours a day and talked with him or her about everything, could there still be something unfinished between you? Answer: *Yes!*

Why? Partially because both the patient and the caretaker are preoccupied during a long-term illness with treatment, comfort, and medication. Partially because it is virtually impossible to talk directly with someone exactly as you would talk to someone else about him or her. And finally, because the death itself provokes an intensity of review that cannot be duplicated while the loved one is still alive. Let us illustrate that point. If you have been involved in a loved one's long-term illness, you will recall that no matter how well you may have thought you were prepared, no matter how willing you were to accept what was going to happen, you were still massively affected when the death actually happened. The finality, the absoluteness, of death upgrades what the brain can do in its search for unfinished business.

Is divorce the same? Yes and no. Divorce is the death of a relationship as well as the accompanying hopes, dreams, and expectations. Feelings about the end of a relationship can begin long before any legal proceedings are initiated. For some, the feelings start during the trip to a lawyer to start a divorce. For others, the feelings don't click in until the formal declaration of divorce is issued by the state. When the sense of finality kicks in, it unleashes the same powerful search by the brain and the heart for things unfinished. But while death automatically signals the *end* of the physical relationship, divorce *changes* the physical relationship.

HOPES, DREAMS, AND EXPECTATIONS

Death is never a singular event. In addition to the actual death, there is the death of all the hopes, dreams, and expectations about the future. Divorces and other relationship breakups conform to the same idea.

In positive relationships, our hopes and dreams relate to the ongoing experience of being together and all the events that are likely to occur over time. Many couples look forward to retirement. They have extensive plans for traveling and pursuing a whole host of hobbies and recreations. All too often, one partner dies before the couple is able to actualize all of those plans. Many of our other positive relationships contain visions for the future. Those pictures also end with a death.

In negative relationships, there is inevitably the hope that someday we will get some fences mended, or that the other person will apologize for what we believe he or she has done to harm us. Many people grew up in dysfunctional homes, surrounded by alcoholism or other debilitating conditions. As children, they didn't always know there was a different way to live. Sometimes, as adults, they realize that they missed out on a normal, healthy childhood. It is essential that they grieve and complete the pain from their childhood. In effect, they must look backward at what they now realize would have been normal hopes, dreams, and expectations.

Some people have horrible relationships with parents or siblings. Occasionally, they are able to work out their differences and arrive at a new positive relationship. As they reunite, they automatically begin to have normal hopes, dreams, and expectations about the future. Much too often, these rekindled relationships are cut short by an untimely death. "I finally got my dad back. We had so much catching up to do. But he had a sudden heart attack and died before we could really begin to enjoy each other."

It is essential that you understand the power of the unfinished emotions attached to future events. You will see and hear many things that remind you of the plans you had with the one who died, or from whom you are divorced. It is important to complete as much as you can now, to help you in the future when there are other reminders.

THE RELATIONSHIP GRAPH

Soon we will give you instructions for making your relationship graph. We will start by giving you examples.

John's Relationship Graph with His Younger Brother

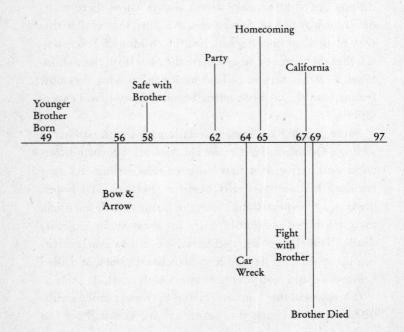

'49—My younger brother is born. It isn't marked above or below the line. That's because I want to tell you a story of poor communication. I'm sure I noticed my mother was pregnant, and I must have asked her what it meant. When she told me it meant I'd have a new brother or sister, I was happy. But I must have been confused because I thought he'd be my size when he arrived. I already had an older brother, so I knew brothers were my size. When they brought him home, I was shocked. He wasn't even big enough to play ball with us. That's my first conscious memory of my younger brother.

'56—My younger brother breaks my bow and arrow. I was angry about it. I'd told him to leave it alone, but he was only seven and wanted to do all the things his older brothers did. I was pretty rough on him and made him cry.

'58—My brother comes to me for comfort and protection. Our parents had been arguing, and he was terrified. He came and crawled into my bed and wanted to know if he could stay with me. I felt very proud that he knew he was safe with me.

'62—I go into the military service. My older brother and younger brother had a going-away party for me. They both told me they loved me and to be safe. I always knew they loved me, but it was nice to hear.

'64—My younger brother wrecks my car. I was overseas and had told him not to use my car. Fifteen-year-olds don't listen well. So one day, when my mother was at work, he decided to go for a ride. The ride ended up a telephone pole.

'65—I come home from the service. When my brother opened the front door, I couldn't believe he had grown so much. He had grown taller than me. He'd become the man of the house. I was proud of him.

'67—My younger brother lives with me in California. If you'll notice, the graph is marked both above and below the line.

We had our ups and downs. He didn't want to come home when I wanted him to. I got to see what it was like to be a parent. He wouldn't make his bed, wouldn't put gas in the car, ran up huge phone bills calling his girlfriend back home. At the same time, we went places together, laughed, and had a great time. He and I became friends as well as brothers.

This was also the year of our biggest argument. He was talking about getting married. I didn't think that was a very good idea. We fought like cats and dogs. He eventually stayed in school and the situation calmed down. I never took the time to clear up the bad feelings.

'69—My brother dies. Our last conversation was over the phone. He and his friends were on their way to visit me in California. They'd stopped for the day and decided to nap. Before doing that, he called me on the phone. The boys were in Las Vegas. They'd never been there before and wanted to see the lights. As usual, he was out of money and wanted to "borrow" some. I told him to go to one of the hotels where I had some friends and they'd give him some money. I hung up after saying, "See you tomorrow."

I never saw him tomorrow. He died that afternoon. How I wished, at the time, that my last conversation had included "I love you." There were other times I wished our conversations had been more feeling-oriented and honest.

John knew and loved his brother for twenty years, but when he did the Relationship Graph for the first time, not many events came to light. When he did start to remember events, at first glance they seemed trivial. Nevertheless, they were associated with the feelings he wished he had acknowledged. It was these undelivered communications he wished had been *different, better, or more.*

We turn now to Russell's Relationship Graph, where the undelivered communications are highlighted in bold.

Russell's Relationship Graph with His Former Wife Vivienne

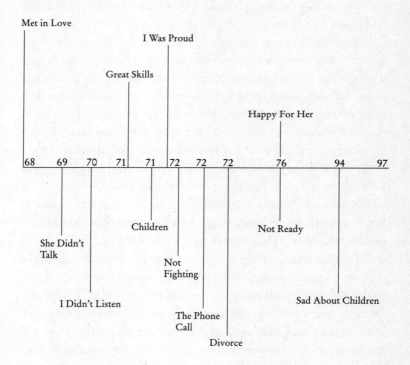

'68—*We meet on a Sunday.* Her name was Vivienne. We married on Tuesday. For me, she was The One. I was smitten. She was very cute. Being from London, she was sophisticated. Looking back, I realize that while she was only nineteen, her English accent and London ways made her seem older to me. I was twenty-five.

'69—Sometimes she appears to be upset with me. My complaint was not that she was upset with me, but how she did or didn't communicate about it. She was always very quiet, but even more so when there was a problem. **I had to forgive her for her unwillingness and inability to tell me what was going on.** I often felt in the dark, and I resorted to guessing what had upset her. It was very frustrating.

'70—I have strong opinions about how we should run our business. I am very verbal and can be self-righteous and dominating. Try as she might, she could not get me to budge off some self-defeating attitudes. She tried to reason with me, but most often I overruled her. Many of the decisions I made in those circumstances led to real business problems later. I have no doubt that they also contributed to our divorce. As I looked at my part of that relationship honestly, I realized that I owed her amends for being overbearing and dogmatic. Not only was I sorry for what happened to me and the business, **but I was genuinely sorry that I had not been able to hear this person who was trying to talk to me and help me.**

'71—Our unique abilities create a nice combination when we open our restaurant together. We were very different people, with different personalities and different skills. I was the friendly host and kibitzer, and she was exceptionally creative with cuisine and baking. **I never took the opportunity to tell her how much I appreciated her skills and the wonderful balance she brought to the business aspect of our lives.**

'71—She wants to have children. Personality issues aside, we did not have too many major differences of opinions or philosophies. We were mostly in agreement about what we were doing and where we hoped it would lead—except in one major area. Vivienne wanted children. It seemed very important to her. Having struggled so much of my early life, and

finally feeling some freedom, I was not at all ready to have children. **I had to forgive her for any part the issue of children played in her request for a divorce. I also needed to apologize for not knowing and telling the truth about myself sooner.**

During our whirlwind four years together, there was tremendous joy. We entertained and were entertained by celebrities. We were the "toast of the town." It was exciting to be with her at events. Being caught in the energy of our lifestyle and our business, I did not always remember to stop and tell her about the important emotions I was experiencing. While we said the obligatory "I love you" every night, **I didn't tell her how much she meant to me, how proud I was to be seen with her, and how wonderful I thought she was.**

I was usually preoccupied with the daily goings-on in our restaurant. I was not as conscious of what was going on in our marriage. *I have already said that I owed her some amends for my overbearing ways.* It would be unrealistic to look at this relationship and conclude that it was only my part or my flaws that destroyed it. While I needed to apologize for my self-righteous verbal dominance, **I also had to forgive her for her quietness and unwillingness to fight for what she believed in—for giving up and giving in.**

'72—She initiates a divorce. As the marriage progressed, there was great confusion for me. On the one hand, I was blissfully happy and unaware that there was trouble in paradise. We had a successful business and, to the best of my limited awareness, a happy marriage. On the other hand, those problem areas, which I can now see with great clarity, were building up a head of steam. One day my wife called me and announced that she was leaving me and applying for a divorce. That telephone call sticks out in my memory. She did not try to talk to me in person, she did it on the phone. **For**

me, it was another example of how poorly she communicated, and I needed to forgive her for doing it that way.

For me, the divorce was very sudden. In the first several weeks following the divorce, I must have walked and talked, but I remember almost nothing. My only conscious awareness about loss was to *be strong for others*. Now I was the "other," and I did not know what to do. During that time, I had a revelation. It dawned on me that my greatest complaint in the relationship was her unwillingness to talk when there was a problem. On the other hand, I realized that when she did talk, I did not listen. I did not know what to do with this awareness. **It was to be much later before I learned that I needed to forgive her for not talking and apologize to her for not listening.**

The divorce ended the marital relationship. While divorce ends most of the physical aspects of the relationship, the emotional and spiritual aspects continue. In divorce, the emotional and spiritual components often change more radically than they do following a death. In the more than twenty-five years since my divorce from Vivienne, a few notable events have helped me discover some additional incompleteness in my relationship with her.

'76—Vivienne tells me that she and her new husband have adopted two baby boys. Shortly thereafter, she became pregnant and delivered a baby girl. My reaction at the time was very mixed. Of course, I was thrilled for her. I had always believed she would be a fabulous mother. But a part of me was hurt. I recalled some old hopes, dreams, and expectations that I had held when she and I were together. **I needed to forgive her for not waiting for me to be ready for children.**

(There is one last important emotional detail about my relationship to Vivienne. In 1974 I met and married Jeanne. When Jeanne and I got together, her daughter Kelly was five years old. I have been Kelly's dad for a long time now. As such, I have been able to have all of the feeling, associated with being a parent. Kelly is a total joy to me, and I treasure our relationship.)

'94—A dear friend of mine adopts a baby girl and names her Gabrielle. She quickly became Gabi, and even more quickly captured my heart. She was seven months old when she came into my life. I immediately nominated myself as number-one uncle. I even had a baby seat installed in my car. From her very first days here, she had me wrapped around her little, little finger. At first, my girlfriend Alice and I were a little baffled at the attention I was paying to this baby.

One day, while delivering a Grief Recovery Seminar, I started talking about Gabi. The next thing I knew, there were tears in my eyes. I realized what was going on. Kelly had been five years old when she came into my life. I had never had the experience of interacting with an infant. Although I was just the "uncle," I did many things with Gabi. I taught her how to crawl, ride ponies, play jacks, and throw a baseball.

As that revelation sank in, I was struck with a deep awareness of what I had missed with Vivienne. I had not had the chance to be a parent with her. I was saddened. Since I had already made my indirect amends and forgiven her, what was left was the picture of us as parents that I had held in my heart since first meeting her in 1968. **How sad I was that we had not had children together.**

FOURTH HOMEWORK ASSIGNMENT: MAKING YOUR RELATIONSHIP GRAPH

To start your Relationship Graph, both those working as partners and those working alone must have chosen one relationship to work on first. Use a sheet of paper at least 8½ x 11″. Turn the paper sideways and draw a line from left to right across the middle of the page. The left end of the line represents the beginning of the relationship. If you are graphing a parent, that date is probably the same as your dawn of conscious memory. For all other relationships, it is the year you met the person. The right end of the line represents the current year; enter it now. If you are graphing a death or divorce, mark the year of that event in the appropriate place. Relationships do not end with death or divorce.

DAWN OF MEMORY—
THE DEATH OF AN INFANT

If you are dealing with grief caused by the death of a child (stillborn birth, miscarriage, abortion, or sudden infant death syndrome [SIDS]), the dawn-of-conscious-memory event will start a bit earlier than it does in most other relationships. Generally speaking, when a woman realizes she is pregnant, *her emotional relationship with her child begins.* Women also describe a change in their feelings when they feel the first flutter inside their body. For the next few weeks, she is constantly saying to her husband, "Can't you feel the movement?" The husband dutifully puts his hand on her tummy but can't feel anything yet. He finally feels the small kick, and *that's when his emotional relationship begins.* It's an imaginary physical relationship at this point, but it's emotionally real. When John's wife became pregnant with his son (the one who died in 1977) and he felt the first movement, his mind immediately began to create hopes, dreams, and expectations. His child was going to have all the things that he didn't have when he was growing up. Although there was no physical relationship yet, it was emotionally real for both John and his wife.

Throughout this book, we have talked about completing a relationship that actually existed, but with the death of an infant, we need to complete a relationship that was supposed to be but never was. When John's son died, he can remember standing outside the nursery and thinking, "He'll never know all the things I was going to do for him. He's never going to know how much I loved him." These were the hopes and dreams he had that would not be realized because of the death. All parents want to give their children all the things they didn't have while growing up. Once this idea is set, what do you do with the thoughts and feelings if the child doesn't live? This type of problem needs to be completed as much as any other.

Next, go to the beginning and reconstruct the relationship to the best of your ability. Your goal is to identify undelivered communications. Let your memory wander. Mark down whatever pops into your mind. Decide whether events are positive (above the line) or negative (below the line). Your mind may or may not go in chronological order. Identify misunderstandings as well as memorable events. Don't edit or limit. Just recall and note. Honesty and thoroughness are essential. Look back at Russell's comments about the incidents on his graph and the undelivered emotional communications associated with each one.

Do not judge what happened. Don't fall into the trap of trying to intellectualize. We're looking for the feelings you had when these events happened. Keep the graph centered on the relationship. Otherwise, it can shift in focus to other surrounding relationships.

Our suggestion is to set aside about an hour and then start. Try to remember at least ten events to plot. If you get stuck, look back at the examples in the book. They may trigger your own memories.

To maintain truth and accuracy and avoid enshrinement or bedevilment, we recommend that you have at least two events above the line and at least two events below the line. Some of you may find it difficult to allow yourself to remember anything negative about a positive relationship. On the other hand, some of you will struggle to identify positive events in your relationship with a less than loved one. For instance, in our memories of an abusive parent, we typically find it difficult to remember positive aspects of the relationship or to assign a positive value to anything about it. To avoid the danger of an inaccurate, larger-than-life picture, we must take pains to be honest. While a parent may have been abusive at many levels, he or she may also have paid the rent and provided food and clothing. Remembering the positive contributions of an abusive parent is not done to minimize the bad things he or she did, but to allow us to arrive at a truthful portrayal of the relationship. All relationships are made up of good and bad, right and wrong, sweet and sour.

Some relationships are mixed and over time may go from good to bad and back. It is very typical to have a good early relationship with a parent, then some rocky teenage years, followed by an excellent adult relationship. You must review the whole relationship. You probably will discover some aspects of incidents during the rocky periods that were not communicated. Do not think that since your recent relationship was good, all previous problems and incidents had been completed.

You get to be the judge. Do not be influenced by what others might think. A woman in one of our seminars listed as one of her fondest memories the times her daddy took her into a saloon and sat her up on the bar while he drank and joked with his buddies. Others might comment that it was abusive to take a little girl into that environment. Others don't get a vote in your memories of your relationship. All that matters is what is accurate for you.

Positive memories can range from sitting together on the porch to going on vacation, holding hands as the sun set, or raising children together. A new dress or toy, swimming lessons, or coaching from a parent might be remembered with tremendous fondness. Do not dismiss a memory because you think it too small. The accumulation of small undelivered communications contributes to incomplete relationships.

An unhappy or negative memory can be as simple as a disagreement. As a child, punishments are often remembered with great intensity. Especially important are those punishments for infractions you did not commit. The unfairness associated with a false punishment often carries lifelong weight. As with the positive memories, no negative memories are too small or insignificant for this exercise.

Use the length of your lines, above and below the horizontal, to indicate the intensity of your feelings at the time the event occurred. It doesn't matter whether there are more events above or below the line; it only matters that what's on the graph is the truth. Don't be concerned with what others will think or say—no one else will see this graph.

Now it's your turn. Begin.

FIFTH PARTNERS MEETING

Congratulations on finishing your Relationship Graph! In this meeting, the partners will share those graphs. Begin by reaffirming your commitments to total honesty, absolute confidentiality, and the uniqueness of your individual recovery. As always, meet in a private place where you will not feel uncomfortable if you cry. Have tissues handy.

Make sure you bring your Relationship Graphs.

Instructions for the Listening Partner
1. Sit a reasonable distance away. Avoid being in your partner's face or smothering him or her.
2. You may laugh or cry, if appropriate, but *you may not talk!*
3. Do not touch your partner. Touch usually stops feelings.
4. Remember the image of being a heart with ears. Do your best to stay in the moment and really listen to your partner's story.

Instructions for the Talking Partner
1. Start by telling the story of the relationship you have graphed, beginning either at your dawn of conscious memory or at the date when you first met the person. Generally, a graph about a parent begins at the dawn of conscious memory, while a graph about a spouse begins in the year you met. Here is an example of each: "I was born in 1943, but my first conscious awareness of my father was in 1947, when I was four years old. I remember him taking me for a milkshake. I had strawberry, and it is still my favorite flavor." "I first met my wife at a friend's party. I'll never forget the feeling of my breath being taken away as I thought how beautiful she was."

2. As you move through the events on your graph, you will intuitively fill in many aspects of the story of your relationship with that person. Be careful not to go off on tangents, especially about other relationships. Also be careful not to turn your story into a monologue. Telling your relationship story should take about half an hour. It's okay to go a little over, but not much. It's most effective to stick to the events you have graphed.

3. If you cry, try to talk while you cry. Push the words up and out, rather than swallowing them. We all tend to choke off feelings in our throats.

4. When you finish telling the story, get a hug from your partner (assuming you've made hugs safe). Both of you should avoid the trap of discussing what you have just done. This is when you run the risk of creating a sense of judgment, evaluation, or criticism.

Take a little break, and then let your partner do his or her graph.

Make your plans for your next meeting.

For Those Working Alone

Since you are working alone, you may find it effective to use John's and Russell's Relationship Graphs as your silent partner. Reread theirs, then look at yours. Notice the similarities and the differences.

12

Almost Home:
Converting the Relationship Graph
into Recovery Components

To communicate and complete the discoveries made in your Relationship Graph, you must first put them into one of the following three categories.

> Amends
> Forgiveness
> Significant emotional statements

As simple as they may seem, these three categories are sufficient to convey any undelivered emotional communication.

AMENDS

Amends are apologies for anything *you did or did not do* that might have hurt someone else. You may owe an amends for something you actually did ("I'm sorry for taking the money from your purse") or for something you did not do ("I'm sorry I didn't visit you in the hospital"). Or you may not have communicated something positive before the death or divorce ("I'm sorry for not thanking you for the present"). In this category, we are primarily concerned with you and your perception of your own actions or nonactions. If you have any sense that something you did or did not do might have harmed or offended the other person, then put it down. It is important to avoid judging yourself. The objective is to become complete, not to hurt yourself further. For the most part, your amends are a private communication between you and your partner. Occasionally, you will discover an amends that can safely be made to a living person. Some amends, however, should and must remain indirect.

VICTIMS HAVE DIFFICULTY WITH AMENDS

Some people develop lifelong relationships with their pain and act like victims. This often becomes a life-limiting and restricting habit. Most people who do this are not aware that it has become an almost automatic reaction to most life circumstances.

It is horrible that anyone is ever mistreated. It is obviously appalling when children, who have no effective means of defending themselves, are mistreated.

"Victims" have a hard time apologizing. The memorized sense of victimhood often creates inaccurate pictures. Nevertheless, there is a need to apologize for your transgressions, no matter how slight, no matter how infrequent. Remember, you cannot be complete with anything less than the whole truth.

Sometimes our desire to be right can be a big problem in making amends. Our sense of rightness or self-righteousness keeps us from being totally honest about our actions and nonactions. Be especially alert to this possibility if you are working on your relationship with a less than loved one. There is a tendency to get caught up in the idea that the other person has harmed you. While true, that does not eliminate your need to make amends for what you have done to them.

FORGIVENESS

Forgiveness is *giving up the hope of a different or better yesterday.*

Forgiveness is one of the least understood concepts in the world. Most people seem to convert the word *forgive* into the word *condone.* The definitions in *Merriam-Webster's Tenth Collegiate Dictionary* illustrate the problem:

FORGIVE: "to cease to feel resentment against (an offender)."

CONDONE: "to treat as if trivial, harmless, or of no importance."

If we believe the two words to be synonymous, it would be virtually impossible to forgive. The implication that we might trivialize a horrible event is clearly unacceptable. However, if we use *Webster's* definition of *forgive,* we are on the right track.

Any memorized resentment of past events will limit and restrict our ability to participate fully in life. Any reminder of the person or event may stimulate a painful reliving of the unfinished emotions attached to it. Successful recovery requires completion of the pain rather than retention of the resentment.

The subject of forgiveness carries with it many beliefs passed on from generation to generation. Some people have developed such a massive resistance to the word *forgive* that they cannot use it. We recently helped such a woman. She called it the "F" word. We gave her the following phrase: *I acknowledge the things that you did or did not do that hurt me, and I am not going to let them hurt me anymore.* A variation is: *I acknowledge the things that you did or did not do that hurt me, and I'm not going to let my memory of those incidents hurt me anymore.*

The insensitive, unconscious, and sometimes evil actions of other people have hurt us. Our continued resentment and inability to forgive hurts us, not them. Imagine that the perpetrator has died. Can your continued resentment harm him or her? Clearly not! Can it harm you? Unfortunately, yes. As with all recovery components, the objective of our actions is to set us free. We forgive in order to reacquire our own sense of well-being. *Forgiveness has nothing to do with the other person.*

Forgiveness Is an Action, Not a Feeling

You cannot feel forgiveness until you do it. Many people say, "I can't forgive him, I don't feel it." To which we say: Of course not. You cannot feel something you have not done. A feeling of forgiveness can result only from the action of verbalizing the forgiveness. Action first, feeling follows.

Forgiveness is giving up the resentment you hold against another person. You may need to forgive them for something they actually did ("I forgive you for ruining my birthday party") or for something they did not do ("I forgive you for not attending my graduation").

There is a strange expression: "I can forgive, but I can't

forget." It mixes two separate ideas that are not directly connected. Imagine that you were horribly beaten over many years. It is not even vaguely possible to forget those incidents. The implication of "I can forgive, but I can't forget" is that, since I cannot forget, I will not forgive. But ask yourself: Who stays in jail? Who continues to resent and shut down his or her own mind, body, and heart? Whose life is limited by the lack of forgiveness?

We are often asked whether, in dealing with living people, it is appropriate to forgive someone in person. Our response is: *NO! NO! NO!* An unsolicited statement of forgiveness is almost always perceived as an attack. The person being forgiven need never know that it has happened. *Remember, never forgive anyone directly to their face.*

One last note: many people ask others to forgive them. We think this is a very incorrect communication. In fact, when you ask for forgiveness, you are manipulating: you are asking the other person to do something that you need to do. And when you ask someone who has died to forgive you, you are asking a dead person to take an action. Spiritual beliefs aside, it is clear that *you need to take an action*, not ask someone else to do it for you. If you are asking for forgiveness, you are really trying to apologize for something you have said or done. Don't try. Do it. Don't ask for forgiveness. Make an apology.

SIGNIFICANT EMOTIONAL STATEMENTS

Any undelivered emotional communication that is neither an amends nor a forgiveness conveniently falls into the catchall category of significant emotional statemens. Here is a list of examples:

I loved you.

I hated you.

I was very proud of you.

I was very ashamed of you.

Thank you for the sacrifices you made for me.

I appreciated the time you spent with me.

This category is both simple and profound. It allows you to convey any and all undelivered communications that have been keeping you incomplete. Although any one statement may appear to be minor, *it is the accumulation of a lifetime of unsaid things that contributes to a sense of incompleteness.*

We have used the phrase *different, better, or more* many times throughout this book. Here is an explanation of that phrase: Following a death or divorce, we almost always discover some things that we wish we had said or done, or some things that we wish that we hadn't said or done. We also remember things we wish the other person had or hadn't said or done. These are some of the undelivered communications that fall into the category, *significant emotional statements.* When relationships end or change through death, divorce, or other circumstances, we almost always have a sense of broken *hopes, dreams, and expectations.* Attached to our awareness of them are significant emotional statements. Now is the time to put words on the thoughts and feelings that the loss robbed us of the opportunity to communicate.

In dealing with living people, it is never appropriate to make a negative significant emotional statement to them. Any negative comment will be perceived as an attack.

❖

Congratulations on finishing your Relationship Graph.

FIFTH HOMEWORK ASSIGNMENT: PUTTING IT ALL TOGETHER

It is now time to translate your Relationship Graph into the recovery components: amends, forgiveness, and significant emotional statements. Take a fresh sheet of paper and set it up as follows:

Amends:

Forgiveness:

Significant Emotional Statements:

Now take out your Relationship Graph. Go through it one event at a time and assign a recovery category to each event. Generally, above-the-line events will be either amends or significant emotional statements. Below-the-line events will be either forgiveness or significant emotional statements. Some events will require two categories, especially negative events. For example: "Dad, thank you for taking me to my ball game" (significant emotional statement). But, "I need to forgive you for telling me that I was the worst player there" (forgiveness).

Many events on your graph will have a corresponding entry in at least one recovery category. Don't be overly concerned if you repeat communications that you think you may have already said to someone. Don't worry if there's more than one event with the same recovery communication. Later you will have an opportunity to refine everything you have done in this exercise. Don't edit. Just get it all down on paper.

SIXTH PARTNERS MEETING

In this meeting, you will share your lists of recovery communications. Begin by reaffirming your commitments to total honesty, absolute confidentiality, and to the uniqueness of your individual recovery. As always, meet in a private place where you will not feel uncomfortable if you cry. Have tissues handy.

Make sure you bring your Relationship Graph and your three lists of recovery categories (amends, forgiveness, and significant emotional statements).

Instructions for the Listening Partner
1. Sit a reasonable distance away. Avoid being in your partner's face or smothering him or her.
2. You may laugh or cry, if appropriate, but *you may not talk!*
3. Do not touch your partner. Touch usually stops feelings.
4. Remember the image of being a heart with ears. Do your best to stay in the moment and really listen to your partner's story.

Instructions for the Talking Partner
1. It is time for you to read your list of amends, forgiveness, and significant emotional statements. There is no perfect

way to do this, but here is one method that works for most. Start with the amends category: "I need to apologize to my father for the times I took money out of his pocket." Or, "I owe my mother an apology for lying to her about staying out late." In this exercise, we are acknowledging the need to make these recovery communications. We will actually make them in our next assignment.

2. Use the same technique with the forgiveness category: "I need to forgive my dad," and so on. Do the same for significant emotional statements: "I need to tell Dad how much . . . ," and so on.
3. If you cry, try to talk while you cry. Push the words up and out, rather than swallowing them. We all tend to choke off feelings in our throats.
4. When you finish your lists, get a hug from your partner (assuming you've made hugs safe). Both of you should avoid the trap of discussing what you have just done. This is when you run the risk of creating a sense of judgment, evaluation, or criticism and of overintellectualizing.

Take a little break, and then let your partner read his or her lists.

Make your plans for your next meeting.

For Those Working Alone

Since you are working alone, you may find it effective to use John's and Russell's Relationship Graphs as your silent partner. Reread theirs, then look at yours. Notice the similarities and the differences in the undelivered communications. Add more if you can. Be thorough.

MOVING FROM DISCOVERY TO COMPLETION

Having taken all of the actions suggested in this book so far, you are now ready to take action to complete the loss. Since the loss you're working on occurred, you have probably become familiar with the pain associated with it. Now is the time to complete your relationship with that pain by completing what is unfinished between you and the person you graphed.

At the suggestion of well-meaning friends or professionals, many people write farewell letters to those who have died. Misinformation is the major stumbling block to recovery. Writing a farewell letter, without proper content, is another piece of misinformation. The origin of the concept of writing a farewell letter is buried in antiquity. Over the past half-century, farewell letters have lost their primary motive of completion. Sadly, they often are merely a recitation of events and emotions, much like a newsletter. People who have written such letters report a measure of short-term relief, but no long-term benefit. We've talked with people who wrote a farewell letter but did not take all the actions outlined in this book. All such attempts at completion have been unsuccessful. To be successful, it is essential to convert the work you have done into a *completion* letter rather than a *farewell* letter or newsletter.

FINAL HOMEWORK ASSIGNMENT: THE GRIEF RECOVERY COMPLETION LETTER©

The Grief Recovery Completion Letter© will help you become complete with everything about the relationship that has been unfinished for you until now. The letter allows you to keep fond memories and all positive aspects of the relationship. You can also keep your beliefs about heaven and other spiritual principles.

You will now be able to say good-bye to what is incomplete. You will be able to say good-bye to any pain you associate with this relationship, including any unmet hopes, dreams, and expectations. You can also say good-bye to the unrealistic expectation of getting something from someone who could not or would not give it. It is most important to remember that good-bye signals the end of this communication, *but that it is not the end of the relationship*.

It is finally time to write your Grief Recovery Completion Letter©. We don't want this letter to be an unsuccessful attempt at recovery for you. It's not a good idea to discuss what you're doing with others. Friends and relatives may mean well, but they haven't read what you've read. They haven't done the work you've done. Please pay close attention to these instructions on what to say and how to proceed.

General Instructions

Writing the letter is best done alone, and in one complete session. Writing the letter can be an emotionally painful experience, and there is too much temptation to avoid the pain. You've already proven your courage. Use it now to write this letter. Many people have known for a long time what wasn't emotionally complete; they just didn't know what to do about it.

Specific Instructions

Allow at least an hour. The most effective way to write your letter is to have your Relationship Graph and your lists of amends, forgiveness, and significant emotional statements in front of you. Look over the graph and the lists and then write your letter. Your graph and lists may contain many repetitions. It is not necessary to repeat the same recovery communications over and over. Use this letter to consolidate them into the most concise expression possible. Your letter should be primarily focused on the recovery categories.

There is no limit on how much you can write, but the emotional intensity is often lost in volume. This is your opportunity to say the most important unsaid things. Generally, two or three standard pages is sufficient. It is okay to write a little more or a little less. If you write more than five pages, you probably need to consider whether you've turned the letter into a newsletter or if you are repeating the same things.

Writing the letter may or may not be an emotional experience for you. Do not be concerned if it is not emotional. Every griever is different and unique.

Here is a helpful format for your letter.

Dear Dad (use the name or title that best represents how you remember the person),
I have been reviewing our relationship, and I have discovered some things that I want to tell you.

Dad, I apologize for. . . .
Dad, I apologize for. . . .
Dad, I apologize for. . . .

(You will probably list more than three incomplete communications in this section. It is helpful to keep them grouped by category.)

Dad, I forgive you for. . . .
Dad, I forgive you for. . . .
Dad, I forgive you for. . . .

(You will probably list more than three incomplete communications in this section. It is helpful to keep them grouped by category.)

Dad, I want you to know . . . (significant emotional statement).
Dad, I want you to know . . . (significant emotional statement).
Dad, I want you to know . . . (significant emotional statement).

(You will probably list more than three incomplete communications in this section. It is helpful to keep them grouped by category.)

Closing Your Letter

Grief recovery is about completion. In order to complete what you have discovered, you must end your letter effectively.

When you speak to a friend on the phone, you conclude the conversation with the word *good-bye* to signal the end of the conversation. We conclude our completion letter with *good-bye* to signal the end of this communication.

For the vast majority of grieving people, the most effective and accurate closing is simply: "I love you, I miss you. Good-bye Dad."

However, many of you may have difficulty with "I love you" and "I miss you." If those statements are not truthful for you, do not say them. An effective alternative is: "I have to go now, and I have to let go of the pain. Good-bye Dad."

You can create other closing statements based on your unique relationship. What should remain constant are the very last words, "Good-bye Dad." Failure to say good-bye can often negate all the good work you've done. *It is the good-bye that completes the communication.* Do not substitute other words. Not saying good-bye leaves the communication open and runs the risk of leaving you incomplete.

Completion Letter—Examples

To help you gain a clear idea of how to write your completion letter, we will give you examples from the relationships we have graphed. The examples are presented in short form to illustrate how to do it. The original letters were longer.

Here are excerpts from John's letter to his younger brother, who died in 1969.

> *Dear Dennis,*
> *I have been reviewing our relationship and have discovered some things I want to say.*
> *Dennis, I apologize for being so rough on you when you broke my bow and arrow.*
> *Dennis, I apologize for acting like a drill instructor the year you lived with me in California.*
> *Dennis, I apologize for fighting with you about your getting married.*
> *Dennis, I forgive you for wrecking my car.*
> *Dennis, I forgive you for the things you did when you lived with me in California, like not taking care of your room, not putting gas in the car, and running up big phone bills.*
> *Dennis, I want you to know how much I appreciated the going-away party you and Bruce threw for me. I want you to know how much it meant to me that you told me you loved me. Thank you.*

Dennis, I want you to know how proud I was of you.

Dennis, I want you to know all of the things that I would have said had I known that I would never talk to you again. I want you to know how much I loved you. I want you to know how proud (and envious) I was of your incredible ability to just pick up a guitar and play any song you ever heard. I want you to know how proud I was of your athletic skill, especially the pole vaulting.

Dennis, I want you to know how sad I have been, realizing that you were not here to share life with. I would have loved to have seen how your career and family life would have been. I am sad that you did not get to be uncle to my children.

Dennis, I love you, I miss you. Good-bye Dennis.

Here are excerpts from Russell's completion letter to Vivienne.

Dear Viv,

I have been reviewing our relationship and have discovered some things I want to say.

Viv, I apologize for being overbearing.

Viv, I apologize for not listening to you, and for not hearing what you were trying to tell me.

Viv, I apologize that I never told you how much I appreciated your skills, and about the positive things that you contributed to our business. Thank you.

Viv, I forgive you for not telling me what was going on with you.

Viv, I forgive you for not understanding that I was not ready to have children, and for not waiting for me.

Viv, I forgive you for how you ended the relationship.

Viv, I want you to know how proud I was to be seen with you.

Viv, I want you to know that I am positive that you are a fabulous mother. And, from time to time, I have been sad that you and I did not get to be parents together.

Viv, I have to go now,

Good-bye Viv.

IMPORTANT NOTE

Communication of a completion letter is a private and confidential issue. As we have stated, forgiveness and negative emotional statements are never made directly to living people. Russell's letter to Vivienne is presented only to illustrate what you must do. A completion letter should never be sent or read to anyone other than your grief recovery partner.

FINAL PARTNERS MEETING: READING YOUR LETTER

Begin by reaffirming your commitments to total honesty, absolute confidentiality, and the uniqueness of your individual recovery. As always, meet in a private place where you will not feel uncomfortable if you cry. Have tissues handy.

Undelivered emotional communications must almost always be verbalized and must almost always be heard by another living person to be considered a completed communication. We have known people who have done everything we have asked you to do, but have not read the letter to a living person. We know them, because they have shown up at our seminars still feeling incomplete. Many of them read the letters at a grave site but had not had another living person there to hear it.

Our brains are unique and somewhat stubborn. No matter what our spiritual or religious beliefs may be, our unconscious mind demands a living observer to attest to the completeness of our communication. We are not trying to be intellectual or mystical; it is merely our practical experience with recovering grievers that has taught us what works and what doesn't.

Instructions for the Listener

1. Your first instruction is to adopt the image of a *heart with ears*. It is your job to listen and listen only. You may laugh or cry if appropriate, but *you must not talk at all*. Nothing about what you do can imply judgment, criticism, or analysis.
2. Take a position at least a few feet away from the reader. We don't want you in the reader's face; it can be a little intimidating. Let your body be relaxed. You are a friend listening to an important communication.
3. During the letter reading, do not touch the reader at all. At this juncture, touch usually stops feelings. We want this reading to be emotional. The reader will have his or her own tissues handy.
4. There is a very real possibility that you will be affected by listening to what your partner reads. Please let that be okay with you. However, you must keep in mind that this is not about you. So, to a limited degree, you need to control the intensity of your reaction. On the other hand, if tears well

up in your eyes, please leave them there. If you wipe them away, you give the message that tears are bad.

5. Your presence is important to the reader. You must *stay in the moment*, even if your head and your heart want to pull you away. Listen with your heart on behalf of your partner.

6. As soon as the reader says good-bye, immediately offer a hug. You will have a sense of how long the hug should last. Don't rush it. The letter has been a culmination of some very painful work.

7. Remember not to analyze, judge, or criticize. It is not necessarily a good idea to talk about the experience. Talking tends to lead to analysis, judgment, or intellectualizing.

Instructions for the Letter Reader

1. Choose a place that is totally safe for you. Avoid public places.

2. Bring along a box of tissues. There is a high probability that you will experience some strong emotions as you read your letter. Keep the tissues where you can get them. We don't want your listener handing them to you.

3. Before you start reading your letter, close your eyes. Although you have enlisted the help of a listener, your objective is to read the letter to whom it was written. Get a mental image of the person you are completing with if you can.

4. Open your eyes. Start reading your letter. You may or may not have an emotional response to your reading. Either way is okay. If you start to choke up, try to talk while you cry. The emotions are contained in the words you have written. Try to push the words up and out of your mouth. Do not swallow your words or your feelings.

5. When you get to the very end, before reading your good-bye sentence, close your eyes, get an image of the person again, and say your final words. This may be accompanied by many tears. If so, make sure you get the words spoken, *especially the good-bye*.

6. Remember, you are saying good-bye to the pain, and you are saying good-bye to any unfinished business. You are *not* saying good-bye to the fond memories. You are *not* saying good-bye to your spiritual beliefs. Say good-bye to the emotional incompleteness. Say good-bye to the pain, isolation, and confusion. Say good-bye to the physical relationship that you had but that has now ended or changed. Say good-bye and then let it be okay that you cry and let it all out. Also, let it be okay if you do not cry. It is essential that you say good-bye or you will probably remain incomplete.

7. As soon as you finish, ask your listener for a hug. You might want and need the hug to be quite long. Don't cut it short. You may find yourself sobbing for a while. Let that be okay with you. You probably have been holding on to the pain for a while. Don't rush the feelings.

For Those Working Alone

If you have been working without a partner, we are going to encourage you to find someone "safe" to help you, someone who would be willing to listen to your letter. The safe person could be a friend, a family member, a therapist, a clergy person—anyone to whom you could explain some simple guidelines. When you find a willing listener, show him or her the listener's instructions in this chapter. Ask your listener whether he or she is willing and able to follow them exactly. Also ask for a commitment to absolute confidentiality.

Some people never find anyone with whom they feel safe. We do not want to compound the problem by telling you to do something that you cannot or will not do.

If you must read the letter without a living human witness, go ahead. Reading a letter alone to a memento, a picture, or at a grave site, can have value. One helpful idea is to read your letter to a tape recorder. Don't destroy the letter. You might find someone you feel safe with to read it to at a future date.

WHAT DOES COMPLETION MEAN?

Having taken all of the actions and having read your letter, you are 100 percent complete. Completion means that you have discovered and communicated what was unfinished for you in all aspects of the relationship that you have remembered up to this moment. It does not mean that you will never be sad again, any more than you would never be happy again. Completion allows you to return to a full range of human emotions. It means that you don't have to go over the same things again and again.

In your day-to-day life, there will be many reminders of the one who has died or your partner from a marriage that has failed. Your moment-to-moment thoughts and feelings will come with emotions attached. Some of your feelings will be happy, fond, and joyful. Some will be negative, sad, and uncomfortable. This is normal. Do not fight it, just allow it. *If you allow negative feelings to occur without resistance, they will pass.* If you try to hide or bury them, they may become painful.

We suggest that you process every feeling in the moment you have it. But what does this mean and how do you do it?

Imagine that you are standing by a large window next to a giant fish tank at a place like Sea World. You are standing there with a friend, watching the fish glide by. As each fish passes, you have a reaction. First, an incredibly beautiful blue fish swims by. Its fins are like silk gently pushing side to side. You turn to your friend and say, "Wow, have you ever seen anything so gorgeous in your life?" Almost before you finish your question, a massive shark swims into view, jagged teeth glinting in the water. Instinctively, you clutch your heart and step back as if the shark could actually get at you. You say to your friend, "How terrifying! My heart is beating like a drum." And just then a school of teeny silver fish, each hardly as big as your little finger, swarms past. There seem to be at least a thousand of them. They twist and turn as a group, in unison, as if only one brain were controlling them. You are fascinated, and you say, "How do all of them know how to go the same way? How come they don't bump into each other?"

You have just processed every feeling in the moment you had it. In the first picture, you were awed by the beauty of the blue fish. In the second, you were frightened by the shark and the images of destruction it conjured in your mind. And lastly, you were baffled and amazed by the synchronized flow of the school in motion.

In each case, you experienced the feeling, verbalized it, and then moved to the next one. In the fish tank analogy, the movement of the fish keeps you going from one feeling to the next. Sometimes in real life we get stuck on a feeling. Or we keep bringing ourselves back to a feeling we had some time ago. When you become aware that you are looking backward at old feelings, remind yourself to keep watching the fish and respond to the next feeling that arises.

✤

STUCK ON A PAINFUL IMAGE

One of the most painful of all experiences is to have a loved one die violently. You may have seen the accident or the aftermath. You may have seen photos of the scene. Or you may only have the pictures your imagination has conjured up. In any event, for many people the imagery seems constant, as if it will never cease. Some of you may have equally disturbing images of your loved one's final hours, days, or weeks as they struggled through a terminal illness. The devastating nature of some diseases often alters appearance so much that you hardly recognize someone you have known your entire life.

Most people, in trying to help a friend, will tell them not to think about it. That is very nearly impossible. We think it is more helpful to acknowledge that the images and pictures are indeed horrible and painful. We also believe that the griever needs to be gently reminded that they have many thousands of other images as well.

We do not all get to go "gently into that good night," as poetry would have it. A woman tells us of her husband's final night at the hospital, with vivid details. Our response is, "What a horrible final picture that is for you." Then we ask, "Do you remember the first time you saw the man who became your husband?" She says yes, and we say, "Tell us what he looked like that day." And she does.

We all have tens of thousands of images of our loved ones. Some of the images are wonderful and happy. Some are negative and sad. And sometimes the final ones are very painful, as when violence or disease have altered how someone looked. It is unrealistic to tell someone not to remember what they saw or imagined. By acknowledging the discomfort of the final, unpleasant pictures, we allow the remembering of all the other pictures. Each time the ending pictures crop up, they must be acknowledged.

Acknowledging the painful pictures and remembering others does not deny or minimize the painful ones. When grievers are allowed and encouraged to state what they are experiencing, the painful pictures subside more quickly. This leaves more room for the review of the entire relationship, not just the ending.

WHAT ABOUT NEW DISCOVERIES?
COLE'S WINDOW STORY

Here is one of our favorite stories for illustrating how to complete your relationship to new discoveries.

When John's son Cole was eight years old, he and his pals would play baseball in the front yard. John taught the boys to position themselves sideways along the front of the house, so that if they missed the ball, it would not break a window. All went well until one fine day the little boys forgot. Cole unleashed one and smash went the neighbor's picture window.

Upon arriving home, John asked Cole to tell him the truth about the window. Cole explained, as only an eight-year-old can, how the ball happened to break the window. Honking horns, barking dogs, and flashing sunlight all contributed to the drama—plus the fact that Cole and his buddies had forgotten to play across the front of the house rather than toward it.

In the middle of the story, John realized that he had stopped listening and started planning Cole's punishment in his mind. Alarmed by his own thoughts, John asked Cole to take a break and go out and play for a while. John looked heavenward and asked this question: "God, where would I get the idea that I want my son, whom I love, to associate telling me the truth with getting punished?" And in a flash, John had his answer. The image of John's dad popped up in his mind's eye as clear as crystal.

John realized that he had just discovered another piece of unfinished emotional business with his own father. He got a pad and pen and wrote:

> *Dad, I was just listening to my son, who I adore more than I can say. He is one of the grandchildren you never got to meet. As he told me the truth about an event with a ball and a window, I stopped listening to him and started preparing his punishment. But that didn't feel right to me. So I have been doing some soul searching. I have just had a revelation—that by the time I was his age, I had long since stopped telling you the truth. Every time I told you the truth, you punished me, and you punished me hard and hurtfully.*
>
> *Dad, I do not want my son to associate truth with punishment. I have to break the cycle set up by what you did to me. I have to forgive you for hurting me every time I told you the truth. I forgive you so I can be free to do things differently with my son. I forgive you so I can be totally free to tell the truth and live the truth and encourage my son to do the same.*
>
> *I have to go now. I love you. Good-bye Dad.*

Having written the letter to his dad, John felt free to talk to Cole. He talked to him about consequences and then went with him and helped him apologize to the neighbor for the broken window. He set up a little program where Cole and his pals could earn some money to pay for the window. And there was no punishment.

There was one more action necessary for John to be totally complete with the event. The next morning at the Grief Recovery Institute, he asked Russell to turn off the phones and listen. John then read the letter to his dad out loud to Russell. After reading the letter, John got a hug from Russell. John had created a completed communication by having a living person hear the words. Just as we have instructed you in the completion process, we do the same. Each new discovery needs to be completed and verbalized. These actions make room for the next piece to float up to the surface.

13

What Now?

Having taken the action of completion, you've still got more work to do.

Making a Loss History Graph may have alerted you to the fact that you have a few more incomplete relationships to work on. We suggest that you start immediately. Our goal for you is the emotional freedom that results from completion of all prior loss experiences.

Make a list of the relationships that you think are still incomplete. Most people have three or four relationships that can benefit from this process. Remember, your relationships with living people are affected when you remain incomplete. If you have worked with a partner, it is helpful to continue with that person.

The process is much quicker the second time through. You do not have to do a Loss History Graph again. You can start with the Relationship Graph. Remember to reaffirm the commitments to honesty, confidentiality, and uniqueness.

After completing the other incomplete relationships, it is

time to live your life. The principles and actions of grief recovery are your new tool kit for losses, disappointments, and other painful life experiences. Practice them so that they become a new habit.

CLEANUP WORK

After completion, we gain a new perspective. Things look different because we have changed on the inside. Completing our relationship has brought about this change. Since the inside has changed, it will now be necessary to look at the outside. You'll want to adjust your environment to reflect this new inside perspective on the loss.

The first step in your cleanup work will be to look at outside reminders of the loss. Earlier we referred to grievers who hold on to everything that represents the deceased loved one. We called this enshrinement. We hold on to these things when we're emotionally incomplete with the loss. There will now be no need to hold on to all of these objects. Some of the objects won't seem to fit with your new perspective; these are the ones you'll want to dispose of. It is normal to want to keep some things and not be sure about others.

Perhaps helpful friends have told you to just get rid of it all—clothes, mementos, everything. But most of us don't want to get rid of it all. One woman we met told us a story of how she made a mistake in disposing of her husband's effects. Everyone kept telling her she had to get rid of all his things. She wanted to do what was right. So one day she drank four bottles of beer to get up the courage to do the job. In her half-drunken state, she threw away everything. She regretted this action the very next day, but by then it was too late.

Before you rush out and throw everything away, let's make a plan that will work. *When possible, never do any of these chores alone.*

Disposing of Clothes: The Pile Plan

One of the most painful tasks for grievers is deciding what to do with the clothes. One good approach has been called the ABC Plan. This approach can also be used for other personal belongings. It has also been lovingly referred to as the Pile Plan. You'll see why as we go along.

Remember, the objective is to end up with what you want to keep without keeping things you don't need or want. Take all the clothes and put them in the living room. Do we mean physically move all the clothes? Yes, that's exactly what we mean. Go through them one at a time. Make three piles of clothes. If you want to talk about a memory that one of the articles stimulates for you, please do so with the person helping you, or call someone. The piles should be grouped as follows:

> Pile A contains the things you are certain you want to keep.
>
> Pile B contains the things you are certain you want to dispose of. Things to sell. Things to give to other family members. Things to give to charity or the church.
>
> Pile C contains all those things you're not sure about yet. If there is any doubt at all about which pile an item goes in, it goes in pile C.

We are not in a race. We're employing a clear plan that works. As you stand in the room looking at all the clothes, it may dawn on you why some people refer to this as the Pile Plan. Dispose of the piles as follows:

> Put pile A back in the closet.
> Give pile B to individuals, groups, and so on.
> Load pile C into bags and boxes and take them to the garage or the attic.

Then congratulate yourself and thank your friend. One month later, bring all the pile C bags and boxes back into the living room and work the plan all over again. Once again, never work alone! Pile A is for the few things you find that you want to keep. Pile B is for those things you are sure you want to discard. Everything else goes back into the bags and boxes, and back into the garage or attic. Doing this task one more time will accomplish your goal of keeping what you want to keep and not retaining things you don't need. If necessary, do it all over again in three months. Eventually, you will be done.

The New Account Solution

Another problem people have trouble with is the checking account with their loved one's name on it. It's fine if you don't want to change the account name. Yet many spouses find that changing the name generates a desired feeling of independence. Once again, people often attack this problem from the wrong direction. Instead of taking your loved one's name off the checking account, open a new one with just your name. Each month, make sure some of your transactions are done through the new account. In no time at all, you'll have a new pattern established and the old checks will no longer be a constant reminder of the loss. To open the new account, go to the bank with a friend, never alone.

Dealing with Anniversary Dates

Even after all the work you've done, certain occasions will still make you sad. This is because you established a lot of familiar habits with your loved one. The good news is that these times are usually predictable. We call them anniversary dates. They don't stand for conventional anniversaries only. Any day that had significant meaning for you can be considered an anniversary date. Since we almost always know when they're coming, we can prepare for them.

The problem is in keeping your feelings to yourself. There is the temptation to try to handle these sad days alone. Don't do that. It's normal for recovered grievers to feel sad on anniversary dates.

Celebrity Deaths

At this writing, the world is still reeling from the death of Diana, Princess of Wales. Our phones have been very busy. We have been interviewed by national and international media to help them understand the incredible outpouring of grief.

The constant question is, "Why do people have so much feeling about someone they never knew?" The answer is: *They did know her, they just never met her*.

If you will recall, in our comments about the death of a child, we talked about having an emotional relationship with someone we had not yet physically met. We all have emotional relationships with the people we admire. They may be princesses, baseball players, actors, or ballerinas. We all have fantasies of meeting them and spending time with them. We usually never get to meet them, and most of us never write a fan letter. When they die, we are left with some undelivered emotional communications.

Since it is a one-way relationship, you probably do not need to do a Relationship Graph. But write a completion letter. Tell the deceased person how much you appreciated him or her. Tell the person that you are sad you never met so that you could have said so in person. Remember to close your letter with "I love you (if appropriate), I will miss you, Good-bye." If possible, read your letter to a friend.

THE FINAL WORD

We know that many people will read this book, enjoy it, and benefit from it. But they will not take the actions of recovery. We feel honored that you have read and appreciated this book. We would feel even better if you would go back and take the recovery actions, with or without a partner. Please don't allow the experience of reading and understanding to lull you into the idea that you are complete. Completion is the result of action.

The Grief Recovery Institute: Services and Programs

The Grief Recovery Institute and thousands of affiliates offer a variety of programs for grievers. Certified grief recovery personnel facilitate Grief Recovery Outreach Programs in cities large and small throughout the United States and Canada. Programs are beginning in other parts of the world.

The Grief Recovery Outreach Program is designed to assist grievers in completing the pain caused by any major loss. The Outreach Program is ideal for anyone who has difficulty finding a partner to do the work outlined in this book.

Grief recovery certification authorizes the use of our registered trademark. Look for Grief ❣Recovery®. It is your assurance that the facilitator has direct access to us and uses our program as designed.

The Grief Recovery Institute is the training facility for the certification program.

The Grief Recovery Institute conducts intensive seminars for grievers nationwide and provides speakers for a wide variety of organizations.

For information on any of our programs, please contact us.

In the United States:
Grief Recovery Institute
PO Box 461659
Los Angeles, CA 90046-1659
(888) 773-2683

A Note from Our Canadian Partner

*I first met John in the early 1980s. As a funeral director, I
realized that I as well as others in my profession received no
training or formal education in grief counseling. As a
professional group, we were ill equipped to help the grievers
who called upon us following a death. In four and a half
days, John taught me more about people's reactions to death
and, more importantly, what to do about it than in all the
years of formal education and years of experience in funeral
service combined. Never again did I have to ask myself,
"What more could I have done?"*

*In 1989 I approached John and Russell with the idea of
expanding the Grief Recovery Institute into Canada. They
agreed, and in 1990 the Grief Recovery Institute of Canada
opened its doors. For the past eight years, John and Russell
have given their time, love, and support to this organization.
On many occasions, they have appeared in the Canadian
office having flown all night to lend a hand when we needed
them the most. Now, almost ten years later, the Grief
Recovery Institute of Canada and the Grief Recovery
Educational Society (a nonprofit charitable organization)
are a valued resource throughout the country to grievers and
the caregiving community.*

Together we have introduced a process of recovery that actually enhances life in an environment that can so easily limit our ability to participate in life. I know there are a great many people who join me in saying thank you, and we love you.

—Eric J. Cline, Executive Director of the Grief Recovery Institute of Canada

In Canada:
Grief Recovery Institute of Canada
284 Water St. N.
Cambridge, Ontario, Canada N1R-3C4
(800) 916-3224

We also hope that you will visit us on the World Wide Web. Our home page is located at:

www.Grief-Recovery. com

You may also E-mail us at: GRI@Grief-Recovery.com

Acknowledgments

From John:

After twenty years, there are far too many people to thank individually. But there are some from the past who cannot go unmentioned. I would personally like to acknowledge: Tommy Atkinson, Dan Brintlinger, John Borgwardt, Duane Chambers, and Steve and Terry Huston. They must receive special recognition and my personal thanks for the early days. I want to thank Frank Cherry, my first partner, who was there at the start.

This revised edition has its own list of people to thank. They are: Jonathan Diamond, our agent, and Trena Keating, our highly skilled yet fun-on-the-phone editor at HarperCollins.

I need and want to thank my partner and friend, Russell. He is the volunteer who wouldn't go away. Now he is my partner in our mission. We laugh and cry together and somehow manage to keep bringing our message of hope to those who need it the most.

I want to thank both my children. Allison was twelve the

last time I wrote an acknowledgment. During the last ten years, I closed my eyes for what I thought was a short time. When I opened them again, she was beautiful, magnificent, and twenty-two years old. Ten years ago, our son Cole was only six. Once an interviewer asked him if he knew what his daddy did. He thought for a moment and said, "My daddy helps sad people." He was right then, and he's still right. He's now sixteen years old, 6'2", and 190 pounds. I cannot tell you how much I love them both.

I need and want to thank the tens of thousands of grievers who've shared their pain, hopes, and dreams with me. I am honored. Without their honest participation, there is no way the Grief Recovery Institute could have become so successful and reached so many hurting people.

How can I possibly acknowledge and thank my wife, Jess Walton. After my son died, I thought I would never get to experience joy again. Just like so many others, I laughed on the outside while crying on the inside. Then Jess came into my life. She has stood by me through all these years. She has joyfully supported this pioneering effort to help grievers. She's put up with my travel, long hours, and crying people in the living room. She even goes on game shows to win money for her favorite charity, the Grief Recovery Institute, when the phone bill is overdue and out of sight. During all this, she's continued to work in her chosen field of acting. She has won much acclaim from her fans and her peers. We even have two Emmy Awards on the mantel. She is a glamorous person in a glamorous profession, and there's nothing glamorous about what I do. I know she understands how much I love and appreciate her, but I want to thank her and tell her, I love you, anyway.

—*John W. James*

From Russell:

Friends and acquaintances, upon learning what I do, always ask if what I do is emotionally draining. My answer is: "What I do is emotionally uplifting. There are very few things that I can imagine that would fill my heart and soul so completely. Every time I help a grieving person, they feel better. So do I."

The principles and actions of grief recovery have altered my life in many ways. I have never been happier. And when I am sad, I am really sad. All feelings are good. Life is no longer a drudge or something to be endured.

My special thanks and love go to:

> My mom—I miss you
> My dad—my friend
> My life partner, Alice
> My business partner and friend, John W. James
> My daughter, Kelly
> My friend Claudia
> My niece Gabi, and her mom, Liza
> My magnificent twin sisters, Margie and Patti
> My wonderful little brother, Ken
> My two lovely ex-wives, Vivienne and Jeanne
> My personal saint, Victor
> My golf buddies, Laurie, Willie, Frank, and Ken, who have tolerated my mood swings as well as my golf swing
> And all the usual suspects, especially Kathleen and Deb

—Russell Friedman